# TEACHING READING AND LITERATURE, GRADES 4–6

## Standards Consensus Series

National Council of Teachers of English
1111 W. Kenyon Road, Urbana, Illinois 61801-1096

Production Editor: Jamie Hutchinson

Manuscript Editor: Jennifer Wilson

Series Cover Design and Interior Design: Joellen Bryant

NCTE Stock Number 51892-3050

**Library of Congress Cataloging-in-Publication Data**

Teaching reading and literature, grades 4–6
        p.    cm. — (Standards consensus series)
    Includes bibliographical references.
    NCTE stock no. 51892-3050.
    ISBN 0-8141-5189-2
     1. Reading (Elementary)—United States. 2. Literature—Study and teaching (Elementray)—United States.  I. National Council of Teachers of English.  II. Series.
    LB1573.T388  1996
    372.41—dc20                                          96–17940
                                                          CIP

# CONTENTS

# INTRODUCTION

## RATIONALE FOR THE STANDARDS CONSENSUS SERIES

**M**uch attention is given to matters that divide the teaching profession. But when NCTE collected dozens of standards statements, curriculum frameworks, and other key state curriculum documents in order to prepare *State of the States: A Report on English Language Arts Content Standards in Each State,* considerable agreement was evident in many areas of English language arts instruction. Similar consensus is demonstrated in the NCTE/IRA *Standards for the English Language Arts,* the core document that outlines national standards in our discipline.

A heartening fact has emerged from the standards movement, as varied as that movement has been: We are after all a community of teachers who draw upon shared instructional traditions in literature, composition, language, and related areas. Furthermore, in recent years the insight and invention of teachers and teacher educators have built upon those traditions in fascinating ways. The result is a rich body of practice–oriented material that parallels the mounting consensus in the profession.

NCTE has developed the Standards Consensus Series, then, in recognition of the existence of core beliefs about English language arts as revealed in innumerable standards–related documents and classroom ideas generated by teachers. The asssumption underlying the series—and illustrated in it—is that good teachers have long been carrying out English language arts programs and classroom activities that exemplify sound implementation of the commonly held standards. The contents of each volume in the Standards Consensus Series were selected mainly from a database of classroom practice materials. The database materials for elementary instruction were selected by teachers from a larger body of writings previously published by NCTE, mainly in the popular *Ideas and Insights* volume (Dorothy Watson, ed.) and in *LiveWire,* an NCTE periodical for and by elementary teachers and teacher educators that flourished in the mid-80s.

In this volume we have gathered exciting activities that draw students into the wider worlds created in literature. The high value that our profession places on encounters with literature is plain from the sampling of state standards documents quoted here:

> *Alaska:* Students who meet this standard will comprehend meaning from written text and oral and visual information by applying a variety of reading, listening, and viewing strategies.

These include phonic, context, and vocabulary cues in reading, critical viewing, and active listening. (n.p.)

*Colorado:* Students read and recognize literature as an expression of human experience. (4)

*Arkansas:* Students will read to comprehend, respond to, evaluate and appreciate works of literature . . . use prior knowledge to extend reading ability and comprehension. (4)

*South Carolina:* Students become familiar with the rich cultural heritage of language through experiences with literature. By reading and personally responding to a variety of genres, the learner develops into a lifelong and selective reader who enjoys a wide variety of literature. (15–16)

*Alabama:* Students will demonstrate knowledge of the types, periods, and characteristics of literature from diverse cultures and places. (n.p.)

*Massachusetts:* Students connect literature to personal experience and contemporary issues. (67)

*New York:* Students learn a wide variety of literary concepts commonly used in reporting on and discussing literature, including genre (poetry, novel, drama, biography, fable, myth, legend), plot, setting, character, point of view, theme, meter, rhyme scheme, tragedy, and comedy. (22)

*Michigan:* Students will explore and respond meaningfully to classic and contemporary literature and other texts from many cultures that have been recognized for their quality and/or literary merit. (25)

*North Dakota:* Students engage in the reading process . . . read a variety of materials . . . organize prior knowledge of a topic before reading . . . make and confirm/disconfirm complex predictions . . . generate questions while reading . . . use strategies for clarification. (12)

Similarly, the national NCTE/IRA *Standards for the English Language Arts* are rich in references to reading and literature. The standards call for reading a wide range of texts, classic and contemporary, from many cultures and for many purposes. They call for student understanding of literature in various genres and from many periods. They state that students must apply a wide range of strategies in order to comprehend, interpret, evaluate, and appreciate texts, noting the importance not only of learning to make predictions about and monitor what is read, but also of drawing on prior experience and engaging in interactions with other readers and writers. The NCTE/IRA standards clearly recognize the classroom as a rich site for strategy development, personal response, thoughtful analysis, and sheer enjoyment when students read texts—not only print but nonprint texts as well.

The powerful statements of the importance of reading and literature expressed in the standards point to the usefulness of this collection as a key volume in the Standards Consensus Series. Of course, this is not to suggest that this book is of value only to those seeking to establish relationships between standards and instructional practice. Every elementary level teacher of English language arts will find a wealth of lively, academically well-grounded ideas in this volume. Even if there had been no "standards movement" as such, these materials would nonetheless present a profile of exemplary practice worthy of emulation in improving students' enjoyment of and performance in reading and literature.

Surely, the upper elementary years are crucial ones in students' literacy development. The wonder and excitement that younger children experience with literature must be sustained even as students become increasingly sophisticated in literary study. They must learn new strategies for reading increasingly varied materials, receiving feedback from teachers and peers and learning to self-monitor along the way. They must continue to respect their own crisp responses to literature while becoming more analytical and critical of the works they read. They must make connections between literature and life and among the various works they read. They must make richer and more explicit links between disciplines and enhance their understanding of relationships between print and nonprint texts. The upper elementary grades can be a most exciting time for student growth; the teaching and learning experiences in this volume demonstrate how such excitement can be brought to instruction that is relevant to standards embraced throughout the country.

A few comments about the nature of the materials and their organization are in order. Consistent with NCTE position statements and with the texts of many standards documents, most of the classroom practices here do not isolate the teaching of literature as if it were unrelated to the entire range of English language arts skills and topics. The materials in the Standards Consensus Series demonstrate amply that good teachers often do everything at once—asking students to reflect upon and talk about literary experiences, encouraging them to make notes about their readings and discussions in preparation for writing, and finding other ways to weave the language arts together in an integral learning experience.

A North Carolina goals document makes this point especially well: "Communication is an interactive process that brings together the communicator(s), the activity or task, and the situation that surrounds them. It is a constructive, dynamic process, not an isolated event or an assembly of a set of sub-skills. . . Though listed separately, the [North Carolina] goals are not to be perceived as linear or isolated entities. The goals are interrelated aspects of the dynamic process of communication" (46). While the focus of this volume is mainly on teaching fiction, then, the classroom experiences typically exemplify the dynamics of real teaching.

## ORGANIZATION OF THE BOOK

The materials in *Teaching Reading and Literature, Grades 4–6* are grouped in useful ways that will be described below. However, neither the arrangement of materials in this text nor the details of a particular classroom experience are intended to be prescriptive. The arrangement of the three sections is for convenience, not compartmentalization. There is no intention to isolate any particular aspect of literacy instruction from other aspects. Indeed, there is much fruitful overlapping of categories; for example, "Food for Thought" in Section 1 involves using clues to draw inferences and raise questions, but it also makes integral use of artifacts, which are the focus of Section 3. In the latter section, "Survival Units" call for students to create and explain a chart, but discussion and analysis, which are emphasized in Section 2, are part of the unit.

As for the details of the classroom activities, teachers who use this book well will invariably translate the ideas in terms of their own experience. Student populations differ; cookie–cutter activities simply don't work in every classroom environment. Most significant, teachers know their own students and they have sound intuitions about the kinds of ideas and materials that are and are not appropriate in their classrooms. From this solid collection of materials, teachers are invited to select, discard, amplify, adapt, and integrate ideas in light of the students they work with and know.

In **Section 1—Clues, Queries, and Follow–ups** students are encouraged to become creative inquirers. Inquiry is encouraged in many ingenious ways, ranging from an enjoyable cloze activity, to gamelike approaches involving contradicting, predicting, and cannily guessing, to exercises in critical and creative thinking. The teachers who developed these classroom experiences clearly have a powerful sense of how to exploit natural curiosity and direct it towards the goals of literacy instruction.

The more sophisticated entries near the end of Section 1 lead naturally to **Section 2—Responding, Discussing, and Analyzing.** The items here illustrate that personal response can move naturally to interaction, and that analysis can flow from response in well–conceived instruction. Comparing and contrasting of impressions in small groups or response logs results in enjoyably unselfconscious learning, often labelled in educational jargon as intellectual discourse and higher order thinking skills. Collaboration is also encouraged in many of these activities as students question, evaluate, and disagree in nonthreatening discussions of literary works. Familiar literary terms such as theme, character, plot development, and point of view appear in this section, not as speed bumps on the road to literacy but as part of a joyful ride through a world of books and ideas.

The emphasis in **Section 3—Beyond the Printed Text: Artifacts and Performances** is, as the name suggests, on using instruments and objects that link the world of print to other media and symbol systems. There are approaches that seem obvious (if only we could think of them), such as using wooden sticks to teach the meter of poems or selecting an object from everyday experience to symbolize a literary character. There are multidisciplinary games and performances in varying degrees of complexity, from pantomime of lively verbs to drawings based on literary works to full–fledged galas such as a story character parade. Far from being precious gimmickry, classroom experiences like these release the student's imagination and illustrate how multiple intelligences can function in parallel ways in various media.

The preparation of this volume revealed that many topics and concerns found in NCTE's previously published classroom practice materials on reading and literature closely parallel the foci of the state–level standards statements cited earlier in this introduction. In a time of considerable pessimism and discord in education, it is encouraging to find such grounds for consensus in the teaching of English and language arts. In the state and national standards, we find *common goals* for the teaching of our discipline. In the reported practices of the English language arts teaching community, we find *a formidable body of ideas about how to achieve those goals.* The Standards Consensus Series is both a recognition of cohesiveness and a tool for growth in the profession.

Finally, some acknowledgments are in order. First, kudos to the teachers and teacher educators who contributed their thoughtful practices to this collection, mostly via entries in NCTE's *Ideas and Insights* volume and past issues of *LiveWire.* The texts from those works are virtually unchanged, and the institutional affiliations of the teachers reflect their teaching assignments at the time of original publication. A few entries in this volume are from non–upper elementary levels (i.e., from early elementary or middle school teachers, or from teacher educators who work with elementary classroom teachers), but all were judged to be appropriate for upper elementary use by the teachers who reviewed materials from the database.

Issues of *LiveWire* and other publications which were sources for this text have been regularly reviewed by chairs of the NCTE Elementary Section and other members. The teachers who categorized the vast body of materials for inclusion in NCTE's general database of teaching practices are Kathleen Alexis, Alice Osborne, Kathleen Shea, and Susan Sheahan. This text was compiled by NCTE staff editor Jamie Hutchinson.

# REFERENCES

Alabama Department of Education. n.d. *Learning Goals and Performance Objectives.*

Alaska Department of Education. 1994. *Alaska Student Performance Standards.*

Arkansas Department of Education. 1993 Edition. *Arkansas English Language Arts Curriculum Framework.*

[Colorado] Standards and Assessment Council. December 1994. *Model Content Standards for Reading, Writing, Mathematics, Science, History, and Geography.* Final discussion draft.

Massachusetts Department of Education. March 1995. *English Language Arts Curriculum Content Chapter: Constructing and Conveying Meaning.* Draft.

Michigan State Board of Education. September 1994. *Core Curriculum Content Standards and Benchmarks for Academic Content Standards for English Language Arts.* Draft.

New York State Education Department. October 1994. *Curriculum, Instruction, and Assessment: Preliminary Draft Framework for English Language Arts.*

North Carolina Department of Public Instruction. 1992. *Competency–Based Curriculum. Teacher Handbook: Communication Skills, K–12.*

North Dakota Department of Public Instruction. 1996. *North Dakota English Language Arts Curriculum Frameworks: Standards and Benchmarks.*

South Carolina English Language Arts Curriculum Framework Writing Team. February 1995. *English Language Arts Framework.* Field review draft.

# 1 | CLUES, QUERIES, AND FOLLOW-UPS

# | THE SPRINKLED SCRIPT

## WHY

Practice with a modified cloze procedure can be an effective method for increasing risk-taking behavior in readers with limited vocabularies and readers who are overly dependent on substituting the word "blank" whenever they feel uncertain of a word. However, being faced with blank lines where words are expected may seem unnatural or threatening to some students. It may even seem that the teacher is testing them, as if this were a fill-in-the-blank exam. A reassuring explanation to the contrary may convince readers who are sophisticated enough to grasp the rationale behind a cloze procedure.

## WHO

Younger or more suspicious students who feel ill at ease with a cloze procedure

## HOW

Write a short play based on the interests and reading abilities of the students who will be using this procedure, or find an appropriate play already in print. Periodically throughout the script, select a predictable word to omit. But rather than having a blank line fill the space, cover the word with a drop of iodine. (Or if the play is written with a felt-tip marker, a drop of water might be sufficient to smear the word.)

Next, tell the students that they are players in an outdoor summer theater and that they have been handed a script that was written in nonpermanent marker. It is starting to sprinkle outside, and wherever a raindrop hits the paper, the marker runs, making the word become a brown splotch. But they are not worried because they know how to ad lib. (This activity should follow previous creative dramatics activities.) Explain to students that any word can be used where they see a splotch, as long as it makes sense and sounds like normal talking. Tell them that the audience in this fantasy hasn't seen the original script and will never know that they are creating dialogue.

## WHAT ELSE

If the students feel comfortable with this activity and are able to ad lib as needed, explain that this same kind of pretending can be a great help to them when they come to unfamiliar words in reading. They can just pretend that they are in a play and need to ad lib, putting in a word that makes sense and sounds normal. Provide some supervised practice with oral reading, in which praise and encouragement are given for students' attempts to ad lib difficult words. Then they can be encouraged to use this same strategy in their silent reading.

*Margaret Berger, Columbia, Missouri*

# BASEBALL MADE EASY: READING FOR MEANING

## WHY

- To reinforce the value of reading for meaning
- To demonstrate to students how incorrect information causes the reader to reread, rethink, and, if possible, correct the passage

## WHO

Middle and upper elementary students who value flawless oral performance above constructing meaning, or students who read for extrinsic reasons and have no personal interest or investment in the process

## HOW

Begin by displaying baseball cards, a baseball, a bat, and other materials associated with baseball. Suggest that students guess the subject of the reading material. Talk about the game. Find out who the experts among the students are.

Ask the students to form groups of three or four. Give each student a copy of the following material to read. Observe students' reactions to the information.

**Baseball Made Easy**

*Chapter 1: How to Choose a Bat*
The best bat for you will be the easiest one to swing, so be sure to pick a bat that is light. With a light bat you can swing faster, and the ball will not go as far.

*Chapter 2: Batting Stances*
You will have to decide for yourself which is the best way to stand. Choose the way that is most natural to you. Everyone is different, so it is important to try and copy someone else.

*Chapter 3: Base Hits*
It is very hard to hit a baseball. Since it takes a lot of practice, you should not expect to get a base hit every time. The secret is to hit the ball to where it is easiest for the fielders to catch.

*Chapter 4: Running the Bases*
In most Little Leagues, you can't steal bases, lead off, or run before the pitch reaches home plate. However, there are three things to remember:

1. Never run when you hit the ball.
2. Run to first base outside the foul line.
3. Always run past first base. You can't be tagged out as long as you stay in foul territory.

*Chapter 5: Your Glove*
Your glove helps you catch hard-hit balls. With a glove there is no reason to be afraid of the ball. Your glove is meant to catch the ball all by itself. Even the worst fielders need to use only one hand.

Discuss the information given, both accurate and inaccurate. Then ask the groups to rewrite the baseball passage, deleting or changing the false statements. If there are experts in the group, they are to expand the information. Students may want to illustrate their copies of the revised passage.

## WHAT ELSE

Extend this lesson by asking students to select other topics and to write their own short texts containing misinformation. Students exchange papers with another student or in their groups and correct the false statements.

*Laura Kinder, Columbia, Missouri, and Shirley R. Crenshaw, Webster University, St. Louis, Missouri*

# | KEONI

Keoni is an emergent reader of Native Hawaiian ancestry. His primary language is Hawaii Creole English, a nonmainstream variety of English which most people in Hawaii refer to as "pidgin." Keoni has learned many Hawaiian words from his family, although he does not speak the Hawaiian language.

When Keoni entered kindergarten, his teacher noticed that he could tell many stories, especially about camping at the beach with his family. Keoni did not have books at home, and his first exposure to the language of books came in the classroom. Fortunately, Keoni's teacher read her students many storybooks and taught them concepts about print through the reading and rereading of Big Books. Keoni watched and listened closely as the teacher read and pointed to the words. Before long, Keoni was noticing patterns in the language and chiming in on familiar refrains. He was also beginning to attend to the print on the page, noticing the words and the letters within them.

During story reading one morning, the teacher read a fable about a coyote and some crows. The fable included the words *roaches* and *crows*. Some of the children seemed puzzled by these words, so the teacher pointed to the illustrations and asked if the children knew what these animals were. Several children used the terms *cock-a-roach* and *mynah bird*. The teacher praised the children for these observations. She pointed out that *roach* was another word for *cock-a-roach*. She explained that crows were noisy like mynah birds, but were larger and not found in Hawaii.

When the teacher had finished reading the story, Keoni eagerly joined in the discussion. He stated that the coyote was a *niele* (nee-eh´-lay), using the Hawaiian word for nosy. His teacher laughed appreciatively at the connection Keoni had made between his home language and the events in the story. Yes, she said the coyote was a *niele,* or you could say he was *nosy* or *curious.* The teacher showed her approval of the connection Keoni had made and took the opportunity at the same time to teach him the global English vocabulary for expressing the same idea.

Near the end of the discussion, the teacher wrote the words *coyote, roach,* and *crow* on the chalkboard and asked for volunteers to mark what they noticed about the words. Keoni raised his hand, and when he went to the chalkboard, he circled the *c*s at the beginning of *coyote* and *crow.* "Like *Candy,*" he said, referring to the name of one of his classmates. The teacher praised Keoni and said that yes, both words began with the letter *c* which was also the first letter in Candy's name, and that *coyote* and *crow* began with the same sound as well. From this incident, the teacher knew that Keoni was learning about words and letters, as well as about the meanings of stories.

Keoni's teacher praised his hunches and insights about words and stories. This gave him more confidence to reflect on his own thinking about the connections among letters, words, sounds, and meanings, as well as the connections between story characters and the structure of stories. The teacher observed that Keoni was making connections between his home language and the school literacy tasks he was learning.

*Kathy Au, University of Hawaii, Honolulu*

# ONE-SIDED CONVERSATIONS

## WHY

To encourage students' interaction with a text by helping them predict what characters are going to say

## WHO

Students who fail to predict from semantic and syntactic cues

## HOW

Give the student half of a conversation between two people, omitting the dialogue of one of the speakers, as in the sample given below:

"Hello! Hello! This is Harvey."
" . . . "
"I'm very well, thank you. And you?"
" . . . "
"That's good. I'm glad to hear that because I've a favor to ask of
    you. . . . Hello?"
" . . . "
"Well, that doesn't sound too friendly. Heh, heh. I'm only kidding."
" . . . "
"Don't be so anxious. I'm about to tell you. I mean, to ask you. It's
    about that money I borrowed."
" . . . "
"Well, no—I don't exactly have it. But I'm good for it. You know
    that."
" . . . "
"Very funny. But seriously, just as soon as I get myself together,
old  buddy. . . . But about that favor—I was wondering, could I ask
    you for a wee bit more?"
" . . . "
 "Fine! I just knew I could count. . . ."
" . . . "
"No, huh? By that, I guess you mean No. Well, it just goes to show
    you who your friends are!"

Invite the student to read the entire discourse before starting the predicting strategy. Then ask the student to read the conversation aloud and to predict the words, phrases, or sentences that would fit or make sense in the conversation.

## WHAT ELSE

1.  Use conversations from a recently read story. Again omit one side of the conversation and ask the student to supply the missing dialogue.

2.  Play "What If I Had Said This Instead of That?" with the student. Ask how his or her responses might change.
3.  Have a conversation between animals instead of people. The student, again, is to supply the missing dialogue.
4.  Ask a student to attempt to complete the conversation without reading the entire passage. Stress that students should expect to have to make corrections.

*Mary A. Evans, Columbia Public Schools, Missouri*

# | MIND READING

## PURPOSE

- To suggest phrases that fit a story context
- To talk about ways an author decides to end a story
- To predict outcomes orally
- To write outcomes to stories

## MATERIALS

Simple stories, to be told by the teacher

I introduce this activity by sticking a tinfoil star on the end of a yardstick and telling students that when I wave my magic wand, they will be able to read my mind. Then I explain that I am going to start to tell a story. When I stop, they will be able to read my mind and figure out what I am going to say next. I first use several stories that are missing phrases, and then I present several open-ended stories. I select familiar scenes that give ideas for many different endings. Here are a few stories I have used:

### Story 1

My niece will be six years old next week. To celebrate, we're going to _____. (At this point, I ask, "Who can read my mind?" I discuss the possibilities with students, verify or establish that I was thinking about having a birthday party, and go on.) For this special occasion, I'm going to wear _____. We're all going to sing _____. Everyone will eat lots and lots of _____. And after that we will play _____.

### Story 2

I was very hungry when I got home last night, even though it wasn't dinner time yet. I couldn't wait, so I went into the _____. After looking around, I decided to make myself a _____. I was just about to eat it when I dropped the _____. What a mess! I had to get a _____ and a _____. After cleaning up, I decided just to _____.

### Story 3

One day when I was about your age I had a friend over to my house to play. It was raining so we had to play inside. I knew I wasn't supposed to play ball inside, but I was showing off. Well, I threw my new ball a little too hard and the next thing I knew, _____!

When the students are reading my mind and making their predictions, I encourage all answers. I don't tell any student that he or she is wrong, but I try to help students think about how their responses fit the context, which response makes the most sense, and which response is the most interesting or imaginative. Sometimes I ask for more information or say, "That was good mind reading. What else might I have been thinking?"

As I tell a story, I record student answers on the chalkboard. When we complete the story, I go over students' responses and ask them to share reasons for the predictions they made. I want them to become aware of the kinds of questions they asked themselves to come up with their guesses so that they can do the same kind of questioning as they read other stories.

After this initial exercise, I ask students to create short stories with words or phrases missing or with open ends and to share their stories with their classmates, who are to fill in the missing words or complete the stories. (The magic wand seems to help here, too, by encouraging hesitant or shy students to participate.) I also occasionally read aloud an appropriate story or a passage from a book, stop at a preplanned point, and ask students to think of a possible ending and write it down. When students have finished writing and a few volunteers have read their endings aloud, I read the original aloud and we compare it to the endings students invented. Talking about the ones they like best and least and about ways an author decides on an outcome can enhance students' reading and writing.

*Karen Matthews, Adams, Massachusetts*

# GET THE POINT?
# THE AUTHOR'S
# AND THE READER'S

## WHY

Often the expectations of readers do not match the intentions of the author. Students need to know that it isn't a matter of "missing the point," but that their interpretations are valid and might be developed more clearly through discussion with other readers. This discussion may help students recognize the differences and similarities between the intentions of the author and the expectations of the reader.

## WHO

All elementary students who need encouragement in recognizing their own ability to construct meaning from text

## HOW

Have students read a story orally or silently. Encourage them to discuss the events that take place in the story. Write their responses on the board or on the overhead projector. As the list develops, question where each event fits—before or after items already listed.

When the list is complete, pick two events from the list and question the author's intentions. Ask students questions such as the following:

- Why do you think the author chose to put in this event? Why did the author put it in at this point?
- Is there anything you want to ask the author about any of these events? Is there something that is not written in the story that you thought might or should happen?

As students talk about the story, encourage them to focus on any difference in their expectations and the author's intentions.

## WHAT ELSE

Students may wish to take notes on the story and use these notes as they write their own takeoffs on the original story. These writings could be shared with other students to see if they as readers get or miss the point.

*Richard Thompson, Columbia Falls Elementary, Montana*

# | ALL ABOUT ANIMALS

## PURPOSE

- To use class and library resources
- To learn or review animal names and characteristics
- To find exact words to match definitions
- To encounter new words in context
- To cooperate with other students in group work

## MATERIALS

- Copies of the worksheet, the clue list, and the answer key
- Pencils

An animal name activity motivates students to brainstorm what they know about animals either before or after an animal research unit. You'll want to use "All about Animals" with small groups so that students can help one another to look up unfamiliar words, think of animals that match the details on the clue list, make educated guesses that fit the space provided on the worksheet, and research the answers they don't know.

First, divide the class into groups of three or four and give each group one copy of the worksheet. Then give every student a copy of the clue list. Explain that the students within each group are to help each other find the right animal names to fill in the worksheet. Point out that some animal names are written horizontally and some are written vertically. After filling in all the answers that they can by talking among themselves, students may research the other clues using class notes, library books, the dictionary, or the encyclopedia.

To begin, one person in the group should read aloud the list of clues and everyone in the group should write their hunches next to the clues on their own clue lists. Then students can compare notes and decide which answers are the best, which fit in the spaces provided, which may require a spelling check, and which clues may require further research. Students in each group may choose one person to be the scribe and to fill in the worksheet, or they may all take turns filling in answers. Advise students to use pencils only, since they will probably change their minds several times about certain answers.

As groups finish their worksheets, they can obtain from you a copy of the answer key to compare with their answers. And in a final class discussion, students can talk about which answers they already knew, those which they had to research, and the resources they used, and they can list on the board any new words they learned.

*Marina C. Krause, Rancho Palos Verdes, California*

## All about Animals—Answer Key

| Across | | Down | |
|---|---|---|---|
| 1. elephant | 13. wolf | 24. zebra | 36. aardvark |
| 2. lion | 14. crane | 25. tiger | 37. ostrich |
| 3. shark | 15. koala | 26. kangaroo | 38. python |
| 4. frog | 16. wolverine | 27. bat | 39. monkey |
| 5. eel | 17. camel | 28. whale | 40. rhinoceros |
| 6. baboon | 18. snake | 29. elk | 41. deer |
| 7. hippopotamus | 19. rat | 30. boar | 42. leopard |
| 8. toad | 20. giraffe | 31. fox | 43. gazelle |
| 9. boa | 21. owl | 32. gnu | 44. vulture |
| 10. asp | 22. hyena | 33. lynx | 45. eagle |
| 11. crocodile | 23. beaver | 34. alligator | 46. ape |
| 12. hawk | | 35. antelope | |

**All about Animals—Clue Sheet**

Across

1. a huge, four-footed mammal with a trunk
2. a powerful mammal of the cat family
3. a sharp-toothed marine animal
4. a small, tailless, four-legged animal hatched in water as a tadpole
5. a snakelike fish
6. a monkey, usually short-tailed, with a dog-like face
7. a very large, thick-skinned amphibious mammal
8. a hopping amphibian resembling a frog
9. a large snake that crushes its prey
10. a small, poisonous snake of Egypt
11. a large, long-tailed, aquatic reptile
12. a strong, swift-flying bird of prey
13. a wild animal resembling a dog
14. a tall, wading bird
15. an Australian animal resembling a small bear
16. a mammal of Canada and the northern United States related to the sable and the marten
17. a large, four-footed, cud-chewing animal that can store water
18. a reptile without arms or legs
19. a rodent resembling a mouse
20. an African animal known for its long legs and neck
21. a nocturnal bird
22. a scavenger found in Africa and Asia
23. a mammal with strong teeth that builds dams and huts

Down

24. an African animal of the horse family with stripes
25. a large Asiatic beast of the cat family with tawny fur and black cross stripes
26. an Australian animal with a pouch for carrying its young
27. a nocturnal flying mammal
28. a warm-blooded, air-breathing sea mammal
29. a large mammal of the deer family
30. a male swine
31. a wild animal of the dog family
32. an African animal also known as the wildebeest
33. a fierce wildcat with a short tail and tufted ears
34. a large reptile of the crocodile family found in the southeastern United States
35. a large variety of mammals, some deerlike, others oxlike in form
36. an ant-eating mammal with a long snout and slimy tongue
37. the largest living bird
38. a large nonvenomous snake resembling the boa
39. a small, long-tailed primate (in contrast with apes and baboons
40. a massive mammal with one or two hornlike projections on it snout
41. a wild animal with antlers
42. a large, catlike mammal with black spots
43. a small, swift antelope found in Africa and Asia
44. a carrion-eating bird of prey
45. a large bird known for strength and keen vision
46. a large, tailless or short-tailed primate

# ALL ABOUT ANIMALS

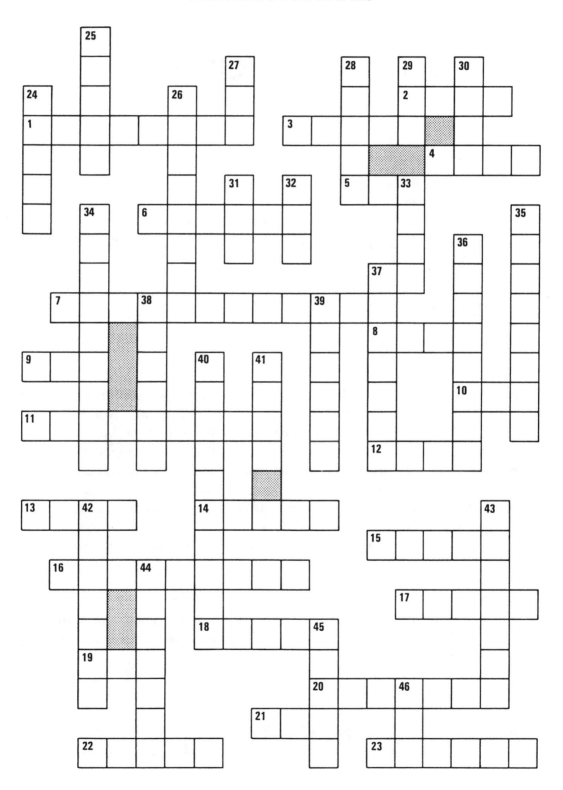

# | FOOD FOR THOUGHT

## PURPOSE

- To read the printed information found on the labels of food containers
- To share unfamiliar words and their meanings with the class
- To exchange questions and answers about why various foods are packaged the way they are

## MATERIALS

- Canned and boxed grocery items
- Dictionaries, paper, pencils

Bring from home a variety of grocery items. A good assortment would include such items as a cereal box, a plastic package of dried fruit, a cylindrical tin of baking soda, a square tin of tea, a spice jar, boxed garlic cloves, a cardboard salt container, several emptied frozen vegetable boxes with the labels attached, a squeeze container of mustard or margarine, a jar of peanut butter, a cake mix, cans of fruit, vegetables, soup in several sizes, etc. The more variety of both content and packaging in the assortment, the more students will have to talk about.

Give one item to each student. Ask students to read labels and find:

- The weight or volume
- The list of ingredients
- Information about special additives, such as "Potassium sorbate added as a preservative" or "Sulphur dioxide used for color retention"
- Instructions on ways to preserve food quality, such as "Refrigerate after opening" or "Keep in a cool, dry place"

Next, students take turns presenting their products to the class and telling their classmates what they learned about the product from the label. A student who comes across an unfamiliar term may look up the term in the dictionary and read it aloud to the class.

Ask students to think and talk about why their product is packaged the way it is. The following questions will start your students thinking: "Why does a cereal box have a plastic liner?" "Why are canned peaches packed in syrup?" "What difference does it make if tuna is packed in oil or water?" "Do you think that your product's package is designed more to protect the contents from moisture or from breakage?" The discussion prompted by this topic may supply some interesting topics for research and writing assignments, such as "Why Food Additives Are Used" and "How to Help Foods Keep Fresh Longer."

*Adapted from an idea by Sandra M. Abbott, Dedham, Massachusetts*

# UNDER THE KITCHEN SINK

What is the most dangerous place in the home? It may be the cabinet under the kitchen sink. Products stored there contain ingredients that may be harmful or fatal to humans. By examining the product labels, children learn the reasons for caution. From the labels they also learn new scientific words, collect information to support their reasoning, and reinforce the good habit of reading print in their immediate environment.

Prepare for this activity by bringing in empty and thoroughly washed containers of products that might be found under the kitchen sink or in other parts of the home. (With spray cans, wind masking tape around the spray nozzle.) The following empty containers (with label warnings and lists of ingredients intact) might be used:

Liquid dishwashing soap bottle
Liquid all-purpose detergent bottle

Crystal bleach substitute box
Spray can of starch
Spray can of soil and stain remover
Liquid bleach bottle
Water softener salt box
Powdered cleanser box
Spray can of furniture polish
Can of powdered bleach and cleanser
Fabric softener bottle
Baking soda box
Ammonia bottle
Liquid toilet bowl cleaner bottle
Crystal drain opener can
Crystal lye box
Spray can of ant and roach killer
Shoe cleaner bottle
Floor wax bottle
Window cleaner bottle
Spray can of air freshener
Spray can of oven cleaner
Spray can of plant bug killer

Each student receives a blank chart with spaces to fill in the product names and the dangers and benefits of each. In pairs or small groups, students talk together about the label warnings and the ingredients in the products.

Allow students to weigh the evidence and to decide from the data whether products could be harmful or fatal. The interaction of students in these groups is important as they work together to identify hazardous products. (Some groups may wish to extend their study of products to include those that children are tempted to eat or drink; they should plan what action needs to be taken if that happens.)

After collecting the data on the products, students can report their findings to the class or to other small groups. Encourage students to make further use of their new information by finding creative outlets. They can prepare a small booklet for younger children, write letters to parents of children in the school to alert them to dangerous products, or create posters for the school halls.

*Aurelia Davila de Silva, Intercultural Development Research Association, San Antonio, Texas*

# | QUESTION THE TEXT

## WHY

Reading with comprehension involves making predictions, asking questions, and then reading to confirm or negate these predictions. When some students are confronted with especially difficult material, they stop active reading—that is, they stop questioning and stop making associations with their own lives. This strategy encourages questioning and active reading, and can also be helpful as a method of note taking.

## WHO

Upper elementary students who are encountering difficult reading material

## HOW

Discuss the reading process with students. One way to do this is to read difficult material aloud and to discuss with students how they can ask questions during the reading. Vary the kind of questions you demonstrate; include statements like "I don't understand the idea of . . . ." Show students how some of these questions can be answered by simply reading further in the selection.

Ask the students to fold a piece of paper vertically. They are to label one side of the opened page "Questions I Have" and the other side "Answers I Can Give." At the top of the page, they list the page numbers of the material they will be reading.

Students begin reading the selection. As they come to things they do not understand or have questions about, they jot down questions in the first column. Encourage them to finish the paragraph or page they are reading before jotting down questions, so that their writing will not interrupt the flow of the reading.

After they have finished reading the entire selection, students return to the questions. Now that they have more information, can they answer any of their questions? Can they answer any by looking at another text?

Encourage them to answer as many of their original questions as they possibly can.

## WHAT ELSE

Students meet with a partner and trade question sheets. First they attempt to answer any of the questions that stumped their partners. Then the paired students look to see if they have any questions that are the same. If so, it may indicate that the author did not do a good job of presenting the material.

This strategy works well both as a beginning for a discussion and as a way to take notes. The class can discuss similar questions and try to brainstorm answers, which may lead students back into the text or to other resource books. Students could keep their pages as notes for reviewing for tests or as notes for writing future papers.

*Carol Gilles, Jefferson Junior High School, Columbia, Missouri*

# | NEXT PAGE, PLEASE

Next Page, Please" is a reading activity with a twist. It requires students to focus on the meaning of the passages they read, but also to think in terms of what they know about how a story fits together. Students receive individual pages from a text; through reading aloud, group discussion, rereading, and group evaluation, they maneuver these disarranged pages into the correct sequence.

In selecting a story to use, choose one that can be understood without looking at the illustrations. Sentences should end on a page and not carry over, and each illustration should cover only one page to avoid giving clues about the correct sequence.

After photocopying each page of the story separately, protect pages from wear and tear with self-adhesive plastic, mix them up, and give one to each student. A volunteer can pass out any leftover pages, and another can collect the pages as the activity progresses.

Each child silently reads his or her page. Anyone who thinks he or she has the first page reads the page aloud and gives reasons for thinking so. If more than one page is suggested, all these pages are read aloud and all reasons are considered. The group decides which page comes first, and the page is passed to the page collector. Don't indicate whether the students are correct or not; that will become clear as the story is gradually reconstructed.

When a decision has been reached on the first page, any student who thinks that he or she has the next page reads that page and gives reasons. Again, all pages are considered, the group makes the decision, and the page goes to the page collector.

This procedure continues as students piece the story together. Encourage them to discuss the sequence as pages are read. When two or more pages are under consideration, have students reread the previous pages and then reread the pages under consideration. Sometimes students discover that a page belongs earlier in the story, or that a page placed earlier in the sequence better fits the current action. Rereading occurs as the change is considered. When all pages have been put in order, the entire story is read aloud by the page collector for a final check on meaning.

This activity is not limited to narrative materials; it can be used successfully with paragraphs of content material, stanzas of poetry, and even notes of songs or steps in solving an equation.

*Karen M. Feather, East Texas State University, Commerce, Texas*

# | SCHEMA STORIES

## WHY

- To convince students that they possess knowledge about the organization of written text and that they should apply this information to the material they are reading

■ To encourage students to become comfortable when reading, to predict the course of the text, and to monitor their own reading

## HOW

By listening to stories of all kinds, children become familiar with story structure (text schema). As they read stories themselves, they bring their own general frame of reference (personal schema) to each new passage. Select passages that have easily identifiable organizing structures, such as beginning, organizational sequence, plot development, climax, and ending. Science, social studies, and math materials may be used, as well as stories from news magazines such as *Scope*, *Sprint*, and *Weekly Reader*. Each section must be long enough to give students something substantial to read.

Cut the passage into three to six sections, depending on its length and complexity. Break the story at highly predictable points so that the student will have schematic and semantic support from the text upon which to predict what the next section will be.

If you are working with a small group of children, give one section of the story to each member. Ask the students to read their sections silently and to think about what must have happened before or after that particular excerpt. Encourage them to think about the similarity of the material to other stories or texts they have read. Is it like a science or social studies text, a play, or a fictional story?

Ask who has the beginning section. That student reads the excerpt aloud and explains why it seems like the beginning of the story. (You may want to leave the title on the section.) Other students indicate whether they agree, perhaps suggesting another section as the beginning of the passage. Proceed through the entire passage, with students making and testing predictions and discussing decisions.

## WHAT ELSE

1. Individual students receive all the sections of the passage and then reconstruct the entire text.
2. Duplicate copies of the passage and give each member of the group all the excerpts to reconstruct. Invite the students to compare the order in which they placed the sections. Discuss how students might come up with more than one acceptable organization for a story.
3. Ask each student to prepare a schema story for the group to reconstruct. The passage may be written by the student or taken from a book or magazine. The student determines appropriate places to break the text into sections.

4. Students use the schema-story procedure as a review of the content-area material.
5. Encourage students to compare the organizing structures of fiction and nonfiction works, possibly written on the same topic.

*Dorothy J. Watson, University of Missouri–Columbia*

# PARTNER BOOK SELECTION

## WHY

Some students often have difficulty choosing books for themselves to read, claiming that they have no interests and don't like to read anything. These same students, however, may be enthusiastic about selecting appropriate books for their classmates.

This strategy provides an opportunity for students to interview other students, so it is especially appropriate at the beginning of the school year as a way for students to learn more about their classmates.

## WHO

Upper elementary students, especially those who have difficulty choosing books for themselves

## HOW

Encourage students to discuss what they need to know about a person before they can select a suitable book for that person to read. As students brainstorm, list their ideas on the chalkboard. They might suggest learning whether the student has any hobbies, if he or she likes to read, how often he or she reads, and what genres he or she prefers. Ask a scribe or a committee to jot down the ideas in a questionnaire form, and make copies of the completed questionnaire for all the students.

Ask students to choose a partner. Students then use the questionnaire to interview each other, recording the answers directly on the questionnaire. Students now go to the library with the completed questionnaires in hand and select one or two books that they feel are appropriate for their partners. Students also choose one book that they would enjoy reading themselves.

When students return to the classroom, ask them to compare their own selections with the partner selected books. The partners might meet again to discuss their reasons for choosing the books. During the silent reading time that follows, students may read from either book, but encourage them to at least sample the partner-selected book.

## WHAT ELSE

1. Many students in one class enjoyed *Little House on the Prairie* and the other books in the series. They wrote to a community resource person who knew a lot about Laura Ingalls Wilder. She responded by volunteering to present a program about Wilder. The class took off with the new idea. Students wrote invitations to other people knowledgeable about Wilder, arranged for them to speak to the class about Wilder, and wrote thank-you notes after the presentation. The program was informative and interested other students in Wilder's books.

2. This strategy can be used in a particular content area, such as social studies. Students devise interview questions that pertain to the content area or narrow their questions to pertain to a certain subject, such as biographies of famous people. Students then find appropriate books for one another related to that subject. Or they might enjoy selecting books that take place within a certain time period, such as in prehistoric times, in the era of medieval knights, or at some future time.

*Carol Gilles and Paul Crowley, Jefferson Junior High School, Columbia, Missouri*

# | THE LITERARY JOURNAL

## WHY

To help students understand what they read and the levels of meaning they encounter

## WHO

All elementary students who are reading short stories, novels, and plays for class or personal reading

## HOW

The following instructions are given to students for developing their literary journals:

1. Use your regular class journal, date each of your entries, and try to write in the journal after each reading session.
2. Without being overly concerned with organization, grammar, usage, spelling, punctuation, or other mechanics, write your personal reactions and responses to the novel or short story. State your thoughts, queries, and feelings on what you read concerning characters, ideas, actions, setting, symbols, plot, theme, and any other aspects of the story that interest you or hold some meaning for you. State what you like or do not like, what you understand or do not understand, what you can identify with, or what seems strange or confusing to you. Hypothesize what may happen or what something means. Draw on personal experiences that connect to the story. It is impossible to be wrong in your responses, so be bold, candid, and genuine, allowing your unique writing voice to emerge. Take risks with your responses.
3. Avoid summarizing what goes on in the story. Instead, react intellectually and emotionally to what you read; then write about it.

4. Occasionally, you may wish to make a drawing about an idea or cut out items from magazines or newspapers that you think relate to the story. If you wish to quote a section of the story and respond—that's fine; do it.

## WHAT ELSE

1. Suggest lead-in sentences only if necessary. My students have come up with the following:

   I'm completely lost at the beginning because _____, but I will read more to _____.
   I wonder what _____ means; maybe I'll find out later.
   I really don't understand what's going on here because _____.
   I feel that this character is just like _____ because _____.
   I remember a time in my life that is similar to this situation in the story; it occurred when _____.
   I can (can't) really understand or identify with what is going on here because _____.
   I know (met) a person just like _____.
   I like this section of writing in the story because _____.
   This section of the story is particularly effective because _____.
   I think the relationship between _____ and _____ in the story is interesting because _____.
   I think this part is weird because _____.

2. Students could later share their journal entries with groups or the whole class or use their journals to review past readings, to stimulate more formal writing, or to foster discussion in conferences.

*Frances E. Reynolds, Rock Bridge High School, Columbia, Missouri*

# 2 | RESPONDING, DISCUSSING, AND ANALYZING

# | TEXT SETS

## WHY

To encourage students to share and extend their comprehension of two or more stories that have similar characteristics

## HOW

Two different procedures may be used that encourage children to share and extend their comprehension of text sets. For both procedures, select two or more stories that feature similar characteristics. See the suggested reading list at the end of the activity for examples of characteristics and text sets that feature the characteristics.

### Procedure A

1. The set of texts is read by everyone for the purpose of identifying similarities across texts. Students may read the texts independently, or you may read a portion of the texts aloud to all the students and then ask students to read the remainder independently.

2. In a group, students discuss the texts' similarities (and differences, if appropriate). Questions to lead off the discussion should be deliberately open-ended, such as the following:

   What was the same about these stories? (narrative)
   What information did you find presented in more than
      one of the stories? (expository)
   What are the similarities in the way these stories were
      written? (expository)

3. After eliciting all possible thoughts about the similarities of the texts, ask the students to identify which of the similarities are of major importance. Ask if they have read or heard other texts that also share the major similarities. (The lesson may end here, or it may continue with steps four and five.)

4. Ask the students, individually or in groups, to write their own texts based on the major similarities in the texts discussed in class.

5. As children complete their rough drafts, ask them to share their new texts with others; invite group comments. Comments should focus on how the child has utilized the major similarities of the previously discussed texts in his or her writing.

## Procedure B

1. Each individual in the group reads a single book from the text set and prepares to share what he or she read and learned from the text with other individuals in the group.
2. Ask each child in turn to relate to the other group members what he or she read and learned. Then invite the others in the group to ask questions, especially those that will help clarify what has been stated.
3. Encourage the children to discuss the similarities and differences across texts as these become apparent.

## SUGGESTED READING LIST
### Books with Similar Stories

**Variations of the Popular Folktale about the Three Little Pigs**

Barbara Brenner, *Walt Disney's The Three Little Pigs*

Paul Galdone, *The Three Little Pigs* (multiple copies available in most libraries)

Donivee Laird, *The Three Little Hawaiian Pigs and the Magic Shark*

Eric Blegvad, illus., *The Three Little Pigs*

**Variations of La Fontaine's Fable about the Miller, the Boy, and the Donkey**

Mary Calhoun, *Old Man Whickutt's Donkey* (written in dialect)

Roger Duvoisin, *The Miller, His Son, and the Donkey*

Lloyd Alexander, *The Four Donkeys* (the book contains a different set of human characters than the two previous stories, but it has a number of interesting similarities, especially with regard to the donkey)

**Variations of the Folktale about Jack and the Beanstalk**

Raymond Briggs, *Jim and the Beanstalk*

Walter de la Mare, *Jack and the Beanstalk*

Joseph Jacobs, *Jack and the Beanstalk*

**Variations of the Folktale about a Large, Quarrelsome Family**

Ann McGovern, *Too Much Noise*

Margot Zemach, *It Could Always Be Worse*

Variations of the Folktale about the Woman Who Swallowed a Fly
    Pam Adams, *There Was an Old Lady Who Swallowed a Fly*
    Steven Kellogg, *There Was an Old Woman*
    Alan Mills and Rose Bonne, *I Know an Old Lady*
    Nadine B. Westcott, *I Know an Old Lady Who Swallowed a Fly*

**Books with Similar Themes**
Understanding the Parts Requires Understanding the Whole
    Janina Domanska, *What Do You See?*
    Lillian Quigley, *The Blind Men and the Elephant*
    John G. Saxe, *The Blind Men and the Elephant*

The Value of Individuality
    Tomie de Paola, *Oliver Button Is a Sissy*
    Munro Leaf, *The Story of Ferdinand*
    Daniel M. Pinkwater, *The Big Orange Splot*
    Bernard Waber, *You Look Ridiculous Said the Rhinoceros to the Hippopotamus*
    Taro Yashima, *Crow Boy*

The Grass Is Always Greener on the Other Side
    Eric Carle, *The Mixed-up Chameleon*
    Liesel M. Skorpen, *We Were Tired of Living in a House*

A Useful Resource for Locating Texts That Are Thematically Similar
    C. W. Lima, *A to Zoo: Subject Access to Children's Picture Books* (R. R. Bowker, 1982)

**Books with Similar Structures**
Characters Sequenced from Big to Little
    Marie H. Ets, *The Elephant in a Well*
    Alexei Tolstoy, *The Great Big Enormous Turnip*

Story Based on Repetition
    Paul Galdone, *The House That Jack Built*
    Rodney Peppe, *The House That Jack Built*
    Edna Mitchell Preston, *One Dark Night*

**Similar Types of Books**
"How" and "Why" Stories—Explanations for Natural Phenomena (Narrative "Text Types")
    Verna Aardema, *Why Mosquitoes Buzz in People's Ears: A West African Tale*

Benjamin Elkin, *Why the Sun Was Late* (another version of the previous tale)

Marilyn Hirsh, *How the World Got Its Color*

Rudyard Kipling, *How the Camel Got His Hump; How the Leopard Got His Spots; How the Rhinoceros Got His Skin*

David McKee, *The Day the Tide Went Out . . . and Out . . .*

**Factual Accounts (Expository "Text Types")**

Eleanor Boylan, *How to Be a Puppeteer;* Laura Ross; *Hand Puppets, How to Make and Use Them* (puppets)

Eric Carle, *The Very Hungry Caterpillar;* Marlene Reidel, *From Egg to Butterfly* (insects)

Ruth Heller, *Animals Born Alive and Well; Chickens Aren't the Only Ones* (animals)

**Texts Containing Stories about the Same Characters**

James Marshall, *George and Martha; George and Martha Encore; George and Martha Rise and Shine; George and Martha Tons of Fun*

*Lynn K. Rhodes, University of Colorado at Denver*

# COMPARING FOLK TALES

These students have been involved in a study of Asian countries. During the related literature studies, the class has been reading Asian folk tales.

As part of the introduction to the story, *Yeh Shen,* the teacher asks the students to meet in small groups and recall the story of *Cinderella.* The small groups then contribute orally to a listing and sequencing of the major components of the story, including the characters, setting, and plot of the story.

The students are now introduced to *Yeh Shen*. After time to preview the book, the teacher has the students meet again in their small groups to accomplish the reading of the story. In this manner, the more capable readers are able to assist those second-language children who are not yet reading, and also those in the class who are not fluent readers. The core literature is open and presented to all the students.

When the reading is completed by most groups, the students are again called together while the teacher leads a discussion of the story, drawing out comparisons between the two stories, defining terms, and clarifying vocabulary with the students.

Upon completion of the discussion, the students are introduced to the Venn diagram form and proceed to establish a Venn comparison of the two tales. This work is completed independently, using the *Yeh Shen* text and the previously listed facts from *Cinderella*.

An extension lesson can include written comparisons of the stories.

*Margaret E. Dewar, Parklane Elementary School, Stockton, California*

Literature Response Logs

# MAKING MEANING, NOT BORROWING IT

## WHY

Reading literature reflects experience and is an experience in itself. When the teaching of literature is approached as a meaning-construction process, readers take ownership of interpretation. If readers feel that the "true" meaning must be explicated to them by teachers and literary critics, they may abandon literature, feeling that understanding is beyond their grasp. In this activity young readers can examine their own perspectives in terms of other points of view.

## WHO

Upper elementary students who think that responses to literature in the classroom involve answering "comprehension questions," writing book reports, or trying to find the teacher's or the author's theme

## HOW

The following activity sequence is used when a group of students reads the same piece of literature. The group can be the entire class or a literature interest group.

1. Each student keeps a reading response log—a notebook with blank pages.
2. The students look at the cover of the book and note its title, author, and illustrator. Then they make predictions about the book in their response logs during a five-minute sustained writing period.
3. Ask students to read to a natural stopping point, such as the end of a chapter or scene. Encourage them to write for five to ten minutes on whatever they are thinking about: their feelings about the reading, questions stimulated by the reading, predictions about what they think will happen next, and so on. The following freewriting is in response to *Sweet Whispers, Brother Rush* by Virginia Hamilton. This response was written after a discussion of the scene in which Tree and Dab, the main characters, leave the apartment for the first time. Scenes from outside the apartment had been described, but except for fantasy travels in time, Tree and Dab had not yet left the apartment. Chris, a student described by many as being of "lower ability," suggested that this meant that Tree was growing up and going out into the world. John, another member of the group, thought that this interpretation made sense and elaborated on the idea in his response:

> I think that Tree is confused because she doesn't know her past and is finally realizing that she has needs and wants and is thinking Dab won't be there for her to take care of and that she has to make something of herself and get a little more active and establish some roots to grow with and expand her thoughts and actions till she realizes that nothing is permanent and that life just keeps on going and you can't afford to fall behind in it and she has to stay on top of things and that no one knows the future and that she has to make one for herself.

4. Students' responses are shared. This discussion helps readers get a sense of what others are thinking about the reading as well as demonstrating that the same text evokes a number of different responses. Accept all responses, but ask students to give reasons for their ideas. "I hate this book" is a legitimate response, but it is incomplete without substantiation.

5. Responses will vary in form as the group gets involved with the book. Questions will be raised, characters will take shape, themes will emerge. Specific topics for responses can be assigned to the group (such as a character's motivation for action). The goal is not consensus, but sharing and considering the ideas of others.

6. As a member of the group, the teacher can present a point of view. Students must understand that this is not "the answer." The teacher's new ideas might stimulate a dying discussion or contribute to a lively one.

7. A final synthesis paper might be written about the ideas expressed in the discussion.

## WHAT ELSE

1. After students finish reading the book, they reread their response logs and write a final entry in which they trace their thought processes, focusing on how their perceptions changed as the reading progressed. Talk about these entries and discuss what it suggests to students about the reading process.

2. Students keep response logs on books they read independently.

3. Keep a response log on books you are reading and share the entries with students.

4. Students publish a collection of their responses along with a synopsis of the book for the classroom or school library.

*Paul Crowley, Jefferson Junior High School, Columbia, Missouri (adapted from an idea by Ben Nelms, University of Missouri–Columbia)*

# INTER-GRADE LITERACY PROJECT

To extend literary experiences in a broader learning community, Mrs. DeMuccio, a fourth-grade teacher, and Mrs. Fludd, a first-grade teacher, initiated an inter-grade literacy project. The two classes would participate in selecting their favorite of ten multi-genre titles nominated for the 1994 Charlotte Award (a literature contest sponsored by the New York State Reading Association). Following their readings, reflections and discussions of the ten books, the fourth graders read the stories aloud to their first-grade schoolmates. In preparation for voting, synopses were written by fourth graders and presented to first graders. Each student then cast a ballot for a favorite story.

Upon learning the results of the statewide vote, Ryan, a fourth grade student, observed that the majority of students in both classes agreed with student voters throughout the state. He wondered why *Martha Speaks* was the favorite. Although Ryan enjoyed the award-winning book, *Martha Speaks* had not been his first choice. Ryan preferred realistic fiction to fantasy.

Curiosity led Ryan to informally question classmates. When he approached Mack (a fourth grader who read *Martha Speaks* aloud to the first graders), Ryan inquired about Mack's opinion and recollections of the first graders' reactions to this story. Mack suggested speaking directly to the other students. The boys collaborated to write interview questions which were posed to individuals from both classes: Which book did you choose? Why? Did you think that *Martha Speaks* would win? Why do you think that so many children voted for it? These interviews were videotaped to be shared.

## INTENT/PURPOSE

Ryan wanted to find out why his opinion was so different from those of most of the other students. His informal inquiries led to the writing of interview questions and implementation of his survey.

## OBSERVABLE BEHAVIOR

Ryan expressed surprise and disappointment when he learned that his favorite book was not the winner. He spontaneously initiated conversations with peers. In those conversations, he attempted to discover the reason for other students' choices. Ryan approached Mack as a resource to gain more insight. Together, they wrote a set of interview questions. This survey was conducted orally and documented on video tape.

## RESOURCES

Curiosity and inquiry are valued in these child-centered classrooms. Students are encouraged to collaborate to explore new ideas and construct meaning. Students in both classrooms benefitted from prior participation in classroom literature discussion groups. These experiences enabled them to internalize and employ sophisticated questioning techniques, such as probing and redirecting, which were first modeled by teachers. Also, students were at ease with responding to open-ended, higher-order questions that involved interpretation and evaluation.

## ASSESSMENT

Ryan demonstrated critical thinking and self-directed learning when he explored the discrepancy between his evaluation versus the evaluations of other students. Through peer collaboration, Ryan and Mack progressed from informal conversation to the creation and implementation of a planned, structured interview. As a result of these interactions, Ryan and Mack gained increased insight and appreciation of others' opinions. The younger students recognized that their opinions held value.

*Forest Park Professional Study Group, Dix Hills, New York*

# | SURVIVAL UNIT

## WHY

- To improve students' reading and writing abilities by exploring a topic through all subject areas
- To enhance students' concept development by actively involving them in the learning process from the beginning

## HOW

This unit involves the study of two or more of the following novels:

Jean Craighead George, *Julie of the Wolves*
Farley Mowat, *Lost in the Barrens;* also published in paper as *Two Against the North*
Scott O'Dell, *Island of the Blue Dolphins*
Armstrong Sperry, *Call It Courage*

The unit lasts approximately three weeks and can be organized in the following ways, depending on the students' interests and the teacher's preference:

1. Four groups of students, each reading one of the novels
2. Two groups of students, each reading a novel from a contrasting region; for example, *Call It Courage* (the tropics) and *Lost in the Barrens* (the Arctic)
3. The teacher reads either *Julie of the Wolves* or *Lost in the Barrens*, students read *Call It Courage* and/or *Island of the Blue Dolphins*

The unit described is designed for four groups, each reading one of the novels. Activities may be ordered so that daily plans include ideas such as the following:

Reading the novel
Discussing the novel

Concept/label (vocabulary) study
Writing an assignment

If the groups are doing different activities at different times, then the teacher will be able to work with each group for part of the time each day. A detailed sequence of activities for this unit follows:

1. The teacher introduces the novels by reading aloud parts of each novel that show the character as lost or alone:

   *Julie of the Wolves*, pp. 5–6
   *Lost in the Barrens*, pp. 58–60
   *Island of the Blue Dolphins*, pp. 39–40
   *Call It Courage*, pp. 21–22

Each of the four groups of students predicts the items that its character will need to survive, and prepares a chart of the predictions. Students then classify the predictions under the basic needs of food, clothing, and shelter and prepare a second chart.

2. After students read the novels, they work in their groups to select details that reveal what the environment is like. Those details are charted under the headings of plants, animals, climate, and geography. Each group determines the setting of its novel and draws a map, using latitudinal and longitudinal lines. Next, students select details from the novels that reveal characterization and the plot. They discuss characterization through a list of directed questions and then write their responses to the questions.

3. The teacher demonstrates how to write "lonethoughts" in the stream-of-consciousness technique, as demonstrated in "Lonethoughts" (Manspace Teacher's Guide, Nelson Stimulus Program, 96–100). Students discuss the loneliness of the main characters in the following sections of the four novels:

   *Julie of the Wolves*, end of Part I
   *Lost in the Barrens*, Chapter 23
   *Island of the Blue Dolphins*, end of Chapter 8
   *Call It Courage*, beginning of Chapter 2

Each group dramatizes its character's thoughts. Students also write the character's thoughts in the stream-of-consciousness technique and arrange these thoughts into free verse.

4. To culminate the study of the novels, students work in groups to prepare and present the following:
   a. A list of survival items used by the character, ranked in order of importance. This chart is compared to the initial chart of survival items.
   b. A chart of basic needs and how the character met these needs. This chart is compared to the initial chart of basic needs.
   c. A map of the character's journey, located as accurately as possible
   d. A drawing or model of the shelter made or used by the character
   e. A time-line of events in the story
   f. A mural of the environment

## WHAT ELSE

1. Students research interesting animals, places, or ideas from the novel. The findings are presented orally, as a poster, or as a written report.
2. Students write another adventure for the main character.
3. Students take on the identity of one of the characters and keep a diary, presenting that character's feelings and his or her perceptions of people and events in the story.

*Ruth Leblanc and Diane Schwartz, Edmonton Public Schools, Alberta, Canada*

# LEARNING ABOUT SELF THROUGH LITERATURE

The class has been reading and discussing pioneer life in preparation for an environmental living experience they will have in December in conjunction with the local historical museum. As part of the process, the children are reading *Little House in the Big Woods* by Laura Ingalls Wilder.

Although the class is very mixed culturally, with about 50% Southeast Asian and the others of various other cultures and ethnicities, a comparison of family life and family celebrations seems to be appropriate.

Upon the conclusion of the chapter detailing a pioneer Christmas with Laura and her family, the class was asked to think about the specific things which made up her Christmas: hanging stockings, special foods, visiting relatives, giving of gifts, and so on. These were detailed and each child looked for specific items to enter in one part of a Venn diagram. Then each child was asked to think of a special celebration from his or her own life and again list the important happenings and material things from that celebration. Now similarities were noted, and moved to the overlapping frame. As the follow-up activity, each child was asked to take his or her Venn diagram and write an informational piece comparing Laura's celebration with their own.

*Margaret E. Dewar, Parklane Elementary School, Stockton, California*

# | READ AND RESPOND

## WHY

To enhance students' comprehension by encouraging response

## HOW

Have students select reading materials that interest them. If necessary, review the guidelines for silent reading time:

1. No one talks.
2. No one gets up.
3. Everyone reads.

Have students read for a set period of time. Then students choose or are assigned partners for shared reading. During this time students read to each other or describe their selections, ask questions, and express their feelings about either selection.

## WHAT ELSE

1. Invite students to respond in writing to either of the reading selections, their own or their partner's. Responses may be in the form of feelings about either book, stories based on ideas from one of the books, evaluations of the book, and so forth.
2. Students form groups of four or five to share written responses. Encourage group members to ask questions about the books or the responses.
3. Students are encouraged to revise their written responses.
4. Students write questions about their partners' books. In small groups, partners then respond to their partners' questions orally or in writing.

*Bill Searcy, Northeast Missouri State University, Kirksville*

Assessment Suggestions For

# LITERATURE DISCUSSION GROUPS

## WHY

The assessment of children's work in literature discussion groups must help both children and teacher move forward in their eager pursuit of intensive and extensive reading, and in their understanding and creating of new knowledge; that is, assessment must help create curriculum. Additionally, evaluation must be in keeping with the model of reading upon which the literature discussion groups themselves are built.

## HOW

Twice during the school year, the literature discussion groups are videotaped. The students and teacher view the tapes and then carefully consider their own roles and contributions to the group. A written evaluation sheet can help direct students' thinking. The teacher and students should work together to create an instrument that the students consider helpful in evaluating themselves. Students need to understand, approve, and suggest items. The form might include the following items:

### Reading and Dialogue

1. As I read the story, I make it make sense.
2. I prepare for the discussion by:
   a. reading the assigned pages
   b. writing in my log
   c. drawing in my log
   d. doing some research
   e. thinking about what I want to say in the group
   f. picking out something in the story or poem to share
3. I relate the story to things that have happened to me.
4. I relate the story to other stories or poems I have read, in terms of the following elements: setting, plot, theme, characters, style, mood, illustrations.
5. I look for patterns in the story and pictures.
6. I connect my ideas with those of other members of the group.
7. I help keep the discussion going by:
   a. staying on the subject
   b. contributing appropriate information
   c. encouraging others

### Participation

1. I listen to other members of the group.
2. I show my attention by looking at the speaker and by responding.
3. I encourage others to speak.
4. I am willing to listen to opposing opinions.
5. I ask for clarification when I don't understand.
6. I speak clearly and loudly enough to be heard by all group members.
7. I speak to all members, not just the teacher.
8. I contribute my fair share to the discussion-- not too much, not too little.
9. I am not easily distracted.

If I am to be graded on the reading and discussion of this book, I would give myself a _____.

Give reasons for your answers if you want to.

## WHAT ELSE

The teacher and students compose questions to be answered either in a short discussion or in written form once a week. Consider some of the following items:

1. The discussions this week were good because . . .
2. Since the beginning of the year the discussions have improved in these ways:
3. The discussions help me understand . . .
4. I have become a better discussion member in these ways:
5. To improve our discussions we should work on . . .
6. I personally need to work on . . .

*Dorothy J. Watson, University of Missouri–Columbia*

# ⏐ SAY SOMETHING

Involve your students in choosing for themselves what is significant in what they read, just as mature readers do. After your students read a passage or story, invite each student to make one significant comment. This might be a statement of agreement or disagreement, a statement of what the student finds most interesting or important in the passage, or a comment on how the passage makes the student feel. Advise students to think carefully about what they want to say, since they may make only one comment each.

Students may choose to make a comment in direct response to the story or, as the discussion evolves, to base a remark on a comment made by another student. For example, a student may begin by saying, "I totally disagree with Tom's statement that . . ."

Students may require a little guidance before feeling comfortable making comments in this setting. Initially, you might suggest that students use statements beginning "This reminds me of . . ."; "When reading this I felt . . ."; or "I liked (or disliked) it when the author said... because . . ." Your students will soon be able to respond with a minimum of cues from you.

*Margaret Atwell, San Bernardino, California*

# SELECTING AND RESPONDING

Early in the school year, books which relate to the theme of study are placed on the book rack. There is a broad selection of titles with each title having from one to five copies. The range of reading level is also broad, encompassing chapter books and picture books, fact and fiction, all relating loosely to the current theme.

Each student is provided a school theme book. He or she will label it as a reading log, decorate the cover, and use the first two pages to begin a list of books read during the year.

The class "shops" the books by placing a book in each student's hands; then, while sitting in a circle, each child spends ½ minute looking at the book and then on a signal passes it to the next person. This continues until each student has seen each book. Then small groups of students are called up and given a choice of what to read and a bookmark for keeping the place.

Now reading time begins, with students free to buddy up and read together, alone, or in pairs. About 25 minutes is given to the reading time at each sitting. As the class matures and becomes more independent, more time may be allotted.

At the conclusion of the reading time, each student writes a reading journal entry in letter form telling the teacher what he or she read and what he or she thought about it. The journals are then turned in and the teacher responds. As the year progresses, these journals also provide the teacher with a time to discuss reading strategies and reading interests with individual students.

One period each week is given to Book Talk. Each student has an opportunity at that time to tell others about what he or she has been reading and to share reading ideas with others in the class.

*Margaret E. Dewar, Parklane Elementary School, Stockton, California*

# | THEMATIC READING

## WHY

Thematic units seek to build understanding of similar ideas found in different reading experiences. Students learn to analyze similarities and differences in themes, characters, and events through well-designed activities, and critical creative readers are able to synthesize a personal response to the theme and to integrate the theme into their own lives. This process of synthesis is one of the higher forms of thought.

## HOW

A thematic unit is simply a reading experience that involves using several books on the same theme. A suggested reading list appears at the end of the activity. Eager readers can be guided toward a few books that approach a theme from many different viewpoints; less avid readers can select books with less disparate viewpoints. After students have read their books, they share their reactions, feelings, and questions in small groups. Then each student selects an activity from the list below:

1. All of the characters are extremely resourceful in handling the tight situations in which they are involved. Construct a master

list of those attributes essential to people who are "on their own."

2. Imagine that all of the characters reach their golden age and retire to a condominium development. They all gather on a community porch to brag about, bitterly remember, or thankfully reflect upon events that shaped their lives, problems that they faced, and how they became successful. Write a eulogy for one of the characters.

3. Write a dialogue between the main characters describing the behavior of one character during a certain event. Try to see that character as they would. How do the main characters feel about him or her?

4. Courage comes in many forms, as demonstrated by the different characters. You are going to present an award at a writers' banquet to the author who created the character displaying the most courage. In a written speech you discuss your reasons for your selection.

5. You are a teacher. Each of the main characters is a student in your class, perhaps at a younger age. The characters' behavior in your classroom is similar to the way they behave in the story. Write a report to each student's parents or guardians explaining how some of his or her behavior is acceptable and how some is quite unacceptable.

## WHAT ELSE

1. After students take a close look at the individuality of the characters, an imagined conversation could be written involving all the individual characters in a particular category. Students could develop a discussion around:

   the relationship characters had with other family members and
       friends
   the person who suffered the most
   the person who helped others the most
   the person who made the biggest discovery
   the person whose invention changed the world the most
   the best ball player in the Hall of Fame

2. If students read several categories of biographies, a more demanding type of synthesis might be appropriate. All the different types of lives read about could be examined for

their common threads, as in the following examples of possible assignments:

a. Write a descriptive formula for becoming one of history's most notable people.

b. Have several famous individuals reflect in writing on their accomplishments in light of the course that time and events have taken. (For example, I doubt if Orville and Wilbur had a 747 in mind.)

c. Use the various categories to develop a hierarchy of most beneficial to least beneficial. Who are the most contributive types of people?

d. From all the individuals studied, select one and nominate him or her for a special Nobel Prize for historical significance. Below are listed some possible categories and individuals in those categories:

*Explorers:* Christopher Columbus, Ferdinand Magellan, Admiral Richard Byrd, Meriwether Lewis and William Clark, Roald Amundsen

*Revolutionary figures:* Patrick Henry, Paul Revere, George Washington, Ben Franklin

*Scientists:* Marie Curie, George Washington Carver, Albert Einstein, Albert Schweitzer

*Inventors:* Alexander Graham Bell, Orville and Wilbur Wright, Henry Ford

*Artists (music, art, sculpture, literature):* Pearl S. Buck, William Shakespeare, Charles Dickens, Elizabeth B. Browning, Wolfgang Amadeus Mozart, Michelangelo

*Sports figures:* Wilma Rudolph, Babe Didriksen, Jim Thorpe, Roger Bannister

*People who have led unusual lives:* Dr. Tom Dooley, Anne Frank, Amos Fortune, Harriet Tubman, Martin Luther King Jr.

*People who have overcome unusual problems:* Helen Keller, Booker T. Washington, Jim Piersall, Henry D. Thoreau

3. After students have read several biographies in one category, plan activities requiring some analysis. The activities should cause a student to look for examples in the various books that illustrate the theme of the category, such as the following activities:

   a. List/discuss/identify essential skills that lead to success in the particular field.

   b. What personality characteristics did the individuals possess that contributed to their success?

   c. Compare the educational and work experiences of the individuals.

   d. What part did fate (accidents, incidents, strange occurrences) play in the development of the individual?

## SUGGESTED READING LIST

### Fantastic Adventuresome Journeys

Lloyd Alexander, *The Book of Three* and sequels

L.Frank Baum, *The Wizard of Oz* and other books in the series, including sequels

Susan Cooper, *The Dark Is Rising* and other books in the series

Roald Dahl, *James and the Giant Peach*

Norton Juster, *The Phantom Tollbooth*

C. S. Lewis, *The Lion, the Witch, and the Wardrobe* and sequels

### Animal Stories

Fred Gipson, *Old Yeller*

Jim Kjelgaard, *Big Red*

Sterling North, *Rascal*

Wilson Rawls, *Where the Red Fern Grows*

James Street, *Good-Bye, My Lady*

### Youth Alone

Robert Burch, *Queenie Peavy*

Felice Holman, *Slake's Limbo*

Scott O'Dell, *Island of the Blue Dolphins*

Conrad Richter, *The Light in the Forest*

Esther Wier, *The Loner*

*Ken Cutts and Patricia Achey-Cutts, Area Education Agency 7, Cedar Falls, Iowa*

# C. S. LEWIS'S *CHRONICLES OF NARNIA*

A reader's special attachment to a book can often be traced to the skillful way in which the author helps the reader to identify with the characters. For this reason (as well as for imaginative detail and the engrossing conflict between good and evil), C. S. Lewis's *Chronicles of Narnia* (Macmillan, 1983) have continued to delight young readers in the years since their publication in 1950. Through discussion and dramatization of the first book of this seven-book series, students gain an understanding of why they identify with certain characters and examine the way the author makes this happen. The seventeen short chapters of *The Lion, the Witch, and the Wardrobe* are equally enjoyable whether you read them aloud in class or ask students to read them at home. (And when this activity is concluded, students will need little encouragement to read the other six books in the series.)

After students have read or listened to you read *The Lion, the Witch, and the Wardrobe,* ask each student to choose a two- or three-page scene that made him or her feel close to a particular character. Students examine their scenes more closely in pairs, comparing thoughts and feelings about the characters they identify with in that scene. For example, if a student identifies with Peter, the student might want to talk about how Peter's relationship with his brothers and sisters compares to the student's own relationship with brothers or sisters. If a student identifies with one of the prominent animal characters, such as Mrs. Beaver or Mr. Tumnus, the student can explain what makes that character seem real. The reader often brings his or her own experiences and background to the story, and this activity helps students to make that connection.

The paired students think of their own questions to ask each other about their characters, in addition to discussing the following questions:

What is this character feeling in this scene?
What is he or she doing?

What memorable words does the author use to show you what the character is doing and feeling?

What additional words or phrases could you use to describe the character's words and actions?

Have you been in a situation in which you felt and acted as this character does here?

What would you do if you were in the same situation as this character?

Next, students have the opportunity to act as their character in their chosen scene, with the freedom to change their character's actions and words as long as the changes fit in with what the character might do and say. Students work with their partners in presenting a scene to the class: the student who chose the scene supplies dialogue for his or her character and uses actions and gestures to show what the character is doing and feeling; the other student acts as the narrator, reading everything except the dialogue spoken by the chosen character.

Sometimes changes in a character's actions and words may mean revising the language used in the rest of the scene. For instance, in the scene where Lucy claims that she found another world inside the wardrobe, a student might identify with Peter and might wish to make Peter either more sympathetic or less sympathetic to Lucy. In dramatizing the scene, the student could change Peter's actions and dialogue to make Peter either more or less understanding. But if such changes in Peter's actions or dialogue are major, the two students will need to use their understanding of Lucy's personality to plan alternate actions and dialogue for her as well.

After each scene presentation, the other students in the class give their opinions as to whether the chosen character is dramatized accurately. If they think that the dramatization fits the chosen character, they explain what cues in the book lead them to think so (for example, the character's previous actions or statements). If they think the words or actions are not in character, they explain why they think that the character would not speak or act in that way.

As students discuss the believability of character portrayals, they become more aware of how an author uses language to develop characters and of how important character development is in making a book meaningful to a reader.

*Susan Lehr, Canal Winchester, Ohio*

# | WHO SAYS?

Looking at point of view in children's books gives students the opportunity to use not only language skills but also critical thinking skills. Telling a story from a point of view different from that of the author is an interesting activity; using a wordless picture book to study point of view can require even more thought and imagination.

When selecting the book, match its complexity to the levels and experiences of your students. You might select a book such as *Hiccups*, by Mercer Mayer, because it has only two characters and the story line is simple and direct. Two hippopotamuses go out on a picnic and ride in a rowboat. The male, elegant in his straw hat, tries to help the female get over the hiccups, and succeeds only when he pushes her out of the boat. Success makes him smug; she is disdainful. Then he gets the hiccups, and she gets her chance for revenge. There are only two points of view to compare, and all of the interaction is between these two characters.

A more complex story would be Mercer Mayer's *Frog Goes to Dinner*. It is the story of a frog who hides in a boy's pocket when the boy and his family go out to dinner. Once inside the restaurant, the frog creates all sorts of havoc, resulting in the family's being thrown out of the restaurant. The boy and frog both appear dejected, at least until they are in the bedroom with the door closed. Then both burst into laughter.

Sixteen characters are in this book (not counting nonparticipants such as restaurant patrons who only watch the action), and thus there are at least sixteen possible points of view for students to examine and develop. In addition, some of the characters witness only certain incidents, which means students could compare viewpoints or produce a joint retelling of the story by different characters.

Once a picture book is chosen, share it first with no purpose in mind but students' enjoyment and understanding. You might decide to share it in small groups, to let students take turns looking at the book, to obtain several copies of the book to pass around, or even to show a filmstrip or motion picture version of the book.

Then ask students to select one of the characters in the book and to imagine that they are that character as they look at the book for a second time. Next, students write what happened from the point of view of that character, including not only descriptions of the action but also what they think the character thought and felt about the events.

When students have finished writing and revising, several volunteers can read their writings aloud. Ask the listeners to talk about how the versions differed and why. This discussion can be followed by an exploration of why people sometimes perceive the same things differently, of the effect of an author's choice of point of view, and of the role and importance of various characters within a story.

*Joan I. Glazer, Providence, Rhode Island*

# | CHARACTER QUESTIONS

## PURPOSE

- to make inferences about characters
- to compare and contrast opinions with other group members
- to reread a text to find support for one's opinion

## MATERIALS

- copies of the handout, page 55
- pencils

In their book *Creative Writing: A Handbook for Teaching Young People* (Libraries Unlimited, 1985), Kathleen Phillips and Barbara Steiner suggest that young authors create a character before they begin writing. Phillips and Steiner provide guidelines for thinking about a character and direct students to determine what the character looks like, what the character likes to eat, where he or she lives and goes to school, and so on. In the process, students get to know the character so well that they don't need to struggle with particulars when they begin to write their stories.

I adapted Phillips and Steiner's guidelines for use with reading assignments to help students understand character development. After reading, I distribute copies of the handout and ask each student to choose a character from the book we read. Students who choose the same character work together in small groups filling out the questionnaires. (It's sometimes necessary to ask for volunteers to switch characters to ensure that each group has enough members.) I tell students that they must be able to explain and back up what they believe about the character. When group discussion brings out differences in opinion about the character, each student must search for specific references within the story to support his or her opinion.

Students are amazed at the amount of information they can learn about a character by reading the text a little more closely. For example, one group of third graders who read Doris B. Smith's *A Taste of Blackberries* (Scholastic, 1976) insisted that they could not know anything about Jamie because "he died by the fourth chapter and isn't in most of the book." However, by the time students had finished discussing the questionnaire and reexamined the text, they had found evidence that he was not only a prankster, but also a caring, fun-loving friend, brother, and son.

Working with the Character Questionnaire will make students more sensitive to the ways authors make their characters seem real. And once students have used the questionnaire in group work, they will be ready to use the questionnaire on their own in both reading and writing.

*Ellen R. Smith, Boulder, Colorado*

## Character Questionnaire

Book Title _____ Author _____

Character _____ Male or Female? _____

1.  Try to picture your character in your mind. What does he or she look like?

Age ____  Height ____  Weight ____  Hair ____  Eyes _____

Other description _____

2.  Where does your character live? How does he or she feel about living there?

3.  Does your character go to school? If so, what grade? Does he or she like school?

4.  Does your character have a job? What does he or she do?

5.  What talents or hobbies does your character have?

6.  What do other characters think of your character? (You can tell by what they say and how they act.)

7.  How does your character feel about himself or herself?

8.  What is the most important thing you can say about your character? Why is it important? How does it contribute to the story?

9.  Circle the words that describe your character:

    | | | | |
    |---|---|---|---|
    | boring | forgetful | mean | polite |
    | careful | funny | smart | understanding |
    | cheerful | gentle | selfish | hopeful |
    | clumsy | kind | shy | sloppy |
    | honest | lonely | silly | secretive |
    | exciting | lazy | happy | curious |

10. Would you like to be friends with this character? Why or why not?

# MAKING HARD CHOICES

aura is a fourth grade teacher in an urban neighborhood; she has 29 students. (Laura's retrospective comments in a teacher discussion group appear in italics.)

Laura read aloud from an early chapter of *Sign of the Beaver,* a historical novel about a young boy whose father leaves him alone in a woodland cabin while he goes to get the rest of their family. Matt has waited for months, facing a series of hard decisions, first whether to let a bearded and hungry stranger into the cabin and later whether to stay long in the increasingly lonely place or go with a new Indian friend, Atean, to his safe village. "What is it like for Matt to be alone? What would you do? Would you go or stay?" the teacher asked the day they read the chapter about Atean. They talked about being home alone themselves, helping out with younger siblings until parents return from work. Laura unrolled a wide roll of masking tape, making a 15-foot line down one side of the room. "This is a decision line . . . if you stand at this end you're deciding to stay in the cabin, but at this end, you're going with Atean. If you were Matt, would you go or stay?"

Children got up slowly and, to her surprise, all 29 children slowly gathered at the "go" end. To get them talking about their reasons she gathered them into groups of four, each with one minute to speak. (*I knew that if they [students with learning difficulties] weren't given that time, the others would kind of eat them up . . . taking the bulk of the time.*) Then they talked more as a whole class, turning back to the book for details about Matt's choice. They imagined what it would be like to leave and be with Atean. (*I let some of the restless ones draw while we talk, when I check on whether they are listening, they most always are.*) The conversation revealed that Laura's students, who face economic stress daily, thought Matt would go so that he could be with people, have food, and be safe. After the discussion, the students listed and wrote about their reasons, and their writing showed those same concerns about isolation and safety. Their writing also showed that the boys were intrigued by the idea of "going on a big hunt" and referred back to details about the Indian belief in the guidance of an animal spirit, or "manitou."

The next day they wrote a new chapter visualizing Matt's first day in Atean's village. There were several students who just sat while others got under way with their writing. Laura walked around, asking several students if she could read their writing out loud. "This is wonderful . . . look what he thought of." *(I modeled a few of them. And then it started clicking, "Oh, that's right, we can do this.")* She encouraged individual children. *(You know how you kneel down and start asking some questions, until your knee locks?)* Little by little, children started writing. *(One of the kids was shy about having his read, so I picked two of them up, juggled them around so that nobody would know whose it was and I read aloud both of those.)* One of her slow starting students "came up with some pretty deep thoughts" writing two pages. *(Now I know that he can do it.)*

Over the next few days, the children talked and wrote stories about other hard choices. A boy who had arrived in the community the year before with his aunt and mother wrote in new English about waiting two years in Cambodia to hear from his father, who had gone ahead to the United States. "And how is this different from Cambodia?" "Were you afraid without your father?" Other students were curious when the boy read his story. The boy's father seemed touched when Laura told him about the story; she waited on the front steps to catch him when he picked up his son. Several other students wrote about how they cope with taking care of siblings until a parent returns from work, and hard decisions they have to make in those situations.

*Catherine Cobb Morocco. Reprinted by permission of Education Development Center, Newton, Massachusetts.*

# 3 | BEYOND THE PRINTED TEXT: ARTIFACTS AND PERFORMANCES

# POETRY AND LEMMI STICKS

**L**emmi sticks" are wooden dowels approximately one inch in diameter and one foot long. As a Girl Scout, I learned to use lemmi sticks to tap out rhythms in a game similar to "Patty Cake, Patty Cake." Recently I discovered that lemmi sticks can be used to help beginning poetry readers develop a sense of rhythm.

I tap out rhythms while reading poems aloud and talk with students about different beats we hear in the poems. To tap out a simple three-beat rhythm, for instance, I hold each stick in a fistlike grip as if I were holding a candle out in front of me; I tap the lower ends of both sticks on the desk or floor, tap the upper ends of both sticks on the desk, and then tap the sticks together, repeating the pattern over and over as smoothly and evenly as possible. Then I distribute lemmi sticks to students so that they can practice tapping out beats as a group, following the rhythm of a simple poem I have copied onto the chalkboard.

When students feel comfortable tapping out rhythms, I may ask them to make up jingles or chants to accompany a particular rhythm. Students might also enjoy choosing poems, coming up with matching rhythms, and beating out the rhythms for their classmates while the poems are read aloud.

*Virginia Irving, Knoxville, Tennessee*

Looking at Things in New Ways
# POETRY AND NATURE

## WHY

Poetry is an excellent medium for promoting close examination. Children carefully examine natural phenomena and then hear poetry that describes these phenomena. Using unusual imagery, the poetry confirms and extends children's original perceptions. Additionally, children develop their linguistic and cognitive abilities as they explore the environment from many different perspectives, using language functionally to accomplish these tasks.

The following activities invite children to hear and respond to a wide variety of poetry, thus experiencing how poets use language to express ideas. Rather than children imitating the form or style of the poetry, the emphasis is on savoring the rhythm, rhyme, and sensory images poetry can evoke. It is only after this observation, exploration, and "playing" with language that students are asked to express themselves in poetic form. Children who have difficulty or lack experience with poetry and writing might require more extensive work with word brainstorming and describing the concrete objects, and might initially prefer writing as a group or with partners.

## HOW

Begin by placing an interesting or unusual object in each of several paper bags. (Possible items to include are rocks with unique textures, shells, particularly pungent smelling herbs, and sandpaper.) Pass each bag around, asking various children to describe the objects without displaying them so that others might guess their identity. Record the descriptive words and phrases. Discuss the various ways each object can be described.

Using books such as *Look Again* and *Take Another Look* by Tana Hoban and *Walk with Your Eyes* by Marcia Brown, ask children to brainstorm words that describe the various natural objects depicted in the photographs. Record their responses on the chalkboard. Discuss the various ways each picture can be described.

Read aloud poetry that describes various objects from nature using unusual imagery. Possible poems to include are "This Is My Rock" and

"Tiger Lily" (David McCord), "Pussy Willow" and "Comma in the Sky" (Aileen Fisher), "Setting in the Sand" (Karla Kuskin), "December Leaves" (Kaye Starbird), "The Tree on the Corner" and "Crocus" (Lilian Moore), and "The River Is a Piece of Sky" (John Ciardi). Ask children to associate the images in the poetry with images from their experiences. Have them suggest other ways to describe these objects.

Next, share poetry that focuses on assuming the perspective of the object or animal being described. *Any Me I Want to Be* by Karla Kuskin and *Prayers from the Ark* by Rumer Godden are excellent collections of poems using this theme. Other poems appropriate for this activity include "Open House" (Aileen Fisher), "Reply to the Question: How Can You Become a Poet?" (Eve Merriam), "Chameleon" (Alan Brownjohn), "The Tickle Rhyme" (Ian Serraillier), and "Great Mouse" (Lilian Moore).

Share poems that associate various sensory images with one word. McCord's "Take Sky" and Kuskin's "Worm" and "Take a Word Like Cat" are good examples to use. Then ask children to create group or partner poems, creating as many associations as they can for one word.

Ask children (either individually or as a group) to go outside and collect their own interesting natural objects. Have each choose a favorite and write a detailed prose description of that object, carefully noting small details and distinguishing characteristics. Students who have difficulty moving beyond the obvious might find that the following guidelines help stimulate thinking:

It looks like . . .

It feels like . . .

It reminds me of . . .

Before I found it, it traveled . . .

It's as big (small) as . . .

Poems that encourage children to think beyond the obvious include Merriam's "Cliché," "Associations," and "Reply to the Question." Children can use materials available in the classroom to illustrate their objects, paying close attention to detail. They could pretend to become the objects they've examined so closely, and write a poem from the perspective of the objects. (Some children may wish to write riddles and then ask classmates to guess the chosen objects.)

A similar set of activities can be completed using ordinary household and classroom objects like safety pins, buttons, paper clips, pads of paper, erasers, and so forth. Excellent poems that stimulate children to view these objects in new ways include "Flashlight," "New Notebook," and "Clockface" (Judith Thurman), "Safety Pin" (Valerie Worth), and "The Garden Hose" (Beatrice Janosco).

## WHAT ELSE

These ideas can be modified for use in examining other topics in unique ways, such as animals, buildings, and signs of the seasons.

*Amy A. McClure, Ohio Wesleyan University, Delaware, Ohio*

# | THE JACKDAW WAY

How can a book about the American Civil War come alive for the readers? From research we learn that the more readers generally "know" about an era, its people, and its places, the more they understand and enjoy what they read. For this reason, a jackdaw can be an answer.

What is a jackdaw? It is a collection of anything, real or imaginary, that concretely relates to the book, time, or theme. The concrete items can range from actual items to imaginary drawings: real food, recipes, clothes or sketches, music or recordings, household gadgets, photographs, poems, maps showing locations in the book, or even biographical sketches of the author and the historical characters. Real or facsimile newspaper articles, shoe box dioramas of important scenes, or timelines from the story can be part of the jackdaw. The maker of a jackdaw is limited only by imagination.

A sample jackdaw might be made for the book *Zoar Blue* by Janet Hickman. This book explores the American Civil War through the eyes of a German community of Separatists—pacifists who discovered the difficulties of remaining neutral while surrounded by war. The items range from real and imaginary objects to background material on the Civil War and on Germans living in Zoar, Ohio:

1. Since the Separatists were not frivolous, corn husks were used for dolls by the young child in the story. A corn husk doll provides a striking contrast with dolls of today.
2. A young boy runs off to enlist in the army where his staple food is hardtack, possibly made from an 1800s recipe. Students who taste this flour and water bread are surprised at the meager fare given to army recruits. Other foods mentioned in the book are made out of cardboard or paper in the shapes of the items they represent.
3. *Uncle Tom's Cabin* by Harriet Beecher Stowe, secretly read by the heroine of the book, is included to alert students to books read in that time.
4. Actual maps (of Zoar and the characters' travels) are included along with researched information on the Separatist way of life.
5. Imaginary diary entries recreate war scenes that did happen or could have happened.
6. Letters exchanged between characters after the war tell about events during the war.
7. A notebook on the Battle of Chancellorsville, so integral to the plot, is included.
8. Sketches recreate the simple clothing worn in the village, the tools used, and the buildings erected.
9. Posters, based on museum pieces, are sketched to reveal attitudes of both North and South.

Jackdaws work when reading about past or present events, and they extend the reader's knowledge and interest for future reading enjoyment.

*Timothy V. Rasinski and Susan Lehr, Ohio State University, Columbus*

# ARTIFACT COLLECTONS
For Literature and Content-Area Reading

## WHY

This strategy is designed to increase students' interest in and comprehension of works of literature and content-area reading selections. This activity is a pedagogical interpretation of schema theory applied to reading. The theory suggests that comprehension is highly dependent upon the background knowledge that the reader brings to the reading act. Artifact collections attempt to develop the reader's background for particular readings.

## HOW

Artifact collections are groupings of various objects that pertain to or are in some way related to a book, a story, a content-area chapter, or any other text that children read. Items that might be a part of an artifact collection include the following:

1. Clothes of particular characters in a book, represented through cutouts from a catalog, paper dolls, or photographs.
2. Songs or music from a place or period of time depicted in the text.
3. Recipes and prepared food typical of the location or time period of the story.
4. Dioramas illustrating certain events from the story.
5. A map showing the locations and journeys depicted in the book.
6. Selected poems that reflect the theme of the reading.
7. A biographical sketch of the author.

The collections can be made up of widely diverse and unusual objects. The only criterion is that the objects be related to the reading selection in some way.

Artifact collections work well when reading literature aloud to the class. At a part of the story where an artifact is appropriate, the teacher or a student can pull the item out of the box, talk about it, and pass it around for everyone to see and touch.

When the class or a group is reading a story together, the artifact collection can be placed in a reading corner for the children to explore on their own. The collection can help satisfy questions that arise when children read, such as "Where is this place?" or "What did that look and feel like?" The collections help bridge the gap between the concrete and abstract.

Several artifact collections can be displayed together in the reading corner with multiple copies of the accompanying books. This can serve as an attractive bait to lure children to books they might not otherwise tackle.

## WHAT ELSE

1. As children become familiar with artifact collections and their corresponding books, they may want to add items to existing collections. Some students may wish to assemble their own collections for books that are personal favorites. This would be an excellent alternative response activity for literature reading, and one that makes the response as fun as a scavenger hunt. Asking students to assemble artifact collections is an alternative way to check their comprehension since they can't prepare the collection unless they've read the book, understood it, and can explain why they selected certain items for their collections.

2. Older students might enjoy making artifact collections for children in lower grades. This activity would be particularly helpful in getting older, less proficient readers involved in books in a purposeful way.

3. Artifact collections could be used to stimulate student writing. Students might be given a particular set of objects from the collection and might be asked to write a story that somehow uses the various objects in an integrated way. Students may wish to compare their completed stories with the text that accompanies the collection.

4. For those classrooms that have separate instruction for spelling, words associated with the artifacts will form a natural spelling unit. In addition to just knowing and spelling the words, the students have the opportunity to touch, see, smell, listen to, and maybe even taste the items associated with those words.

*Timothy V. Rasinski, University of Georgia, Athens*

# | CAPTURING CHARACTER

As part of the term-end culmination before the break in a year-round program, the students are asked to reflect and review the books and stories which have been read by the whole class since the opening of school. As each title is named, the teacher asks for the major characters in that story and lists them on a wall chart divided into boxes, one for each story.

Each student is then asked to think personally about one story character who was special for him or her. Now each student is to list symbols they associate with that special character. Some examples would be a cooking pot for Strega Nona, a cape for Sarah Noble, a doll for Laura Ingalls, a pumpkin or glass slipper for Cinderella, and so on.

Now each student writes about why that particular character was important to him or her and designs a symbolic quilt square for that character in nine patches. Students may complete more than one piece as they so choose. Using characters now in individually read books rather than core literature pieces.

The quilt pieces become part of a character sharing period, with each child displaying and sharing individual work with the class.

*Margaret E. Dewar, Parklane Elementary School, Stockton, California*

# | POEMS AND PANTOMIME

Poetry is the art of choosing words; pantomime, the art of avoiding words. But pantomime, like poetry, compels us to share ideas and emotions, and can also personalize a student's experience of a poem.

In "Poems and Pantomime," students read one or two poems aloud, discuss the words and phrases that they like, and capture the mood and meaning of these phrases in pantomime. In trying to match words and phrases with movement and facial expressions, students learn the subtle differences among words. Students also experience the poem in a more active, involved way than by simply reading and discussing it.

Lillian Morrison's "The Sidewalk Racer" or "On the Skateboard" (from *The Sidewalk Racer and Other Poems of Sports and Motion),* is a good choice for use in this activity. A student volunteer can read the poem aloud to the class before you distribute a photocopy to each student. You'll want to read the poem aloud again while students listen for phrases they like and circle these phrases. Let students know that they will be acting out the phrases they select, and that the easiest words to act out are concrete action words such as *soar, tumble, flutter, slowly, shyly,* and so on.

Question students about their choices. What does it mean to "skim on an asphalt sea"? Where does the "whirring" sound come from? Students can talk among themselves about the movements or emotions suggested in the phrases they chose. For an example, read aloud the line "I swerve, I curve, I sway" and ask students to create a picture in their minds of the shape their bodies take when they "swerve," "curve," and "sway" while on a skateboard. How would they show the differences between these actions? (You may need to remind students that this is still preparatory discussion, not acting out.) How fast would they move? Would they "sway" slowly or rapidly? Would they "swerve" with great force or gently? And how would a student show that he or she was a "sailor and a sail" or a "driver and a wheel" while riding on an imaginary skateboard?

Let volunteers share how they would interpret their own favorite phrases from the poem, and then get ready to pantomime. Students can stand in the aisle by their desks or around the room in a circle. (As a rule of thumb for space allotment, make sure that each student has enough room to extend his or her arms in all directions.) After students "warm up" for a few minutes,

**69**

using an activity such as playing catch with an imaginary balloon, ask them to experiment and find some body movements and facial expressions to match one or two of the phrases that they circled on their poem. As they practice these movements, students can ask nearby classmates to critique their movements and offer advice for making their mime more convincing.

After ten or fifteen minutes, ask for volunteers to pantomime their phrases in front of the class. If students wish, they can pantomime without first reading their phrase aloud, and the audience can try to identify the specific phrase from the poem.

Understanding "sound" words and the differences between them is just as important as understanding words of movement. Kaye Starbird's "The Wind" (from *The Covered Bridge House and Other Poems*) can be used to make this point. At first glance, for instance, my students thought that "gasp" and "cough" meant about the same thing, but as we discussed and mimed these terms, they discovered differences. You may want to ask your students to use mime to show the differences between gasping and coughing. Is one louder? Is one more airy? How can you move your arms and shoulders and neck to show that you are coughing? What is the difference between these movements and those you make when gasping?

To act out phrases from any of these poems, students must integrate their knowledge of the mood and intent of the poem with what they already know about the words used. And although pantomime may not be the students' usual response to reading a poem, this activity will encourage them to feel movement and hear more sounds as they bring their knowledge, senses, and imagination to the words on the page.

*Jeannette Miccinati, Ithaca College, Ithaca, New York*

# | POETRY POSTERS

At no cost but your time, you can cover the walls of your classroom with posters illustrating lines and verses from your students' favorite poems. Your students are the designers and artists as they choose and illustrate lines and verses of poetry from books that you provide, and the finished posters are classroom resources that can be displayed time and time again.

Start by letting students read and color copies of the sample poetry poster on page 72. Have a copy of Henry Wadsworth Longfellow's "The Wreck of the Hesperus" on hand so that interested students can read more of the poem. (And you might mention the date of Longfellow's birthday—February 27)

Then spread out a wide selection of poetry books in a central location and ask students to create their own poetry posters by finding and illustrating a line or verse of poetry that they like. Provide both felt-tip markers and old magazines so that students may choose between drawing and cutting out pictures that relate to their verses.

Make sure that younger students have sheets of drawing paper large enough to accommodate picture and verse. After displaying the posters for a while, file them away to bring out again the next time you're discussing poetry.

*Elizabeth Archer, DeSoto, Illinois*

## POETRY POSTER

She struck where the white and fleecy waves
    Looked soft as carded wool,
But the cruel rocks, they gored her side
    Like the horns of an angry bull.

*The Wreck of the Hesperus*

Reprinted from *Scenes from Longfellow's Poems,* a coloring book drawn by Sandra J. Whitmore. Copyright Maine Historical Society.

# | FANTASY STORIES

This second grade class of 32 students speak little or no English. They are learning to read and write in their native tongue, Spanish, while receiving supplemental instruction in English. So that the students don't fall behind grade level with their English-speaking counterparts and can continue to progress academically, they are instructed in Spanish until their English is fully mastered, and then they can function in both languages.

After reading and discussing the story of "Ramiro," a storyteller whose characters take off on him because of the mean roles he makes them play, the children begin to tell their own fantasy stories. The teacher starts the students off by having them imagine that they are sitting at their kitchen table drawing; then mom or dad calls them to bed. They go to sleep, and when they get up the next morning to have their breakfast, they see that their drawing paper is blank. When they look around for their drawing, they bump into the real thing. Their drawing becomes a three-dimensional reality!

Now the children delight in what they drew and what happened to the drawing when it became real. All kinds of fantastic characters come "alive," from a giant pink chicken running loose in the kitchen to yellow dinosaurs to ghosts, witches and spaceships. The children illustrate their fantasies, and based on the oral interaction they write out the story. After editing, they bind and "publish" their work and share their books with one another.

Because of the wide range of skill levels in this group, the students who complete their projects first work cooperatively with those who are still emergent readers and writers. These students express their thoughts orally while their partners write them down. Each student then copies his own work. The children not only derive enjoyment from their reading, but it is also used as a springboard for writing activities relating them to real-life experiences. Working cooperatively, they progress at their own speed.

Being able to orally express feelings and thoughts reduces the frustration of the low achiever while being able to attain the same end result as the others (with help from a peer)—a finished story project.

*Olga G. Roesch, Princeton, New Jersey*

# | FOOLED AGAIN

Fourth-grade students, ages 9–10, small class group. Students read and role play the story "Rabbit and the Tiger." There are four characters: the storyteller, a rabbit, a tiger, and farmers. Rabbit tricks the tiger and makes him go to the bottom of the lake, thinking there is cheese on the bottom. The tiger almost drowns, but comes out of the lake alive. Afterwards, the tiger tried to find the rabbit to eat him, but the rabbit ran away, since he is faster than anything.

After the students role play the story, they write down different occasions in life where they can be fooled by others. The following day, students act out the story using their own characters and relating the story to their daily lives.

This story is very effective for ESL students (students that are also in a Bilingual classroom) because they get to express themselves and experience the richness of literature. Students develop a positive attitude not only for reading but for reading in English.

*Olga Fitzgibbons, Princeton, New Jersey*

# STORY CHARACTER PARADE

## PURPOSE

- To share information about favorite books and authors
- To participate in a parade dressed as a book character

## MATERIALS

- Clothes and other materials suitable for use in dressing up as book characters

Creating a parade of favorite story characters is a project appropriate for a single class or a whole school. The guidelines below were developed when this project was used with students in grades 1–5 as part of a celebration of Children's Book Week in the fall, but a story character parade could be adapted to various purposes. For instance, it might be developed as an alternative to traditional book reports, used to culminate a unit in children's literature (biography, folklore, historical fiction, etc.), to highlight books read for a special occasion (Black History Month, RIF Day, etc.), or to highlight the works of a particular author.

## INTRODUCING THE ACTIVITY

Introduce the project at least two weeks in advance to allow time for planning and preparation. After explaining the nature of the project to students, be ready to provide answers for such questions as these:

Does my character have to be from a book I have already read? (We ask students to look for characters in books already read so that preparations can begin right away.)

Does the book have to be one I have read in school? (As long as a copy of the book can be obtained and the chosen character is appropriate, we allow students to select books read outside the class.)

Can I be a cartoon character or one from television or movies? (We limit our parade to book characters.)

Can I be an animal or object like a tree? (We allow this as long as the animal or object is an important character in the book.)

If you decide to invite parents to attend or even to help with the parade, invitations or notices are best sent home as soon as you begin preparations. To help students visualize the possibilities for selecting a character and planning a costume, display books that contain illustrations of different types of story characters, such as *Where the Wild Things Are, The Little Engine That Could, The Little House on the Prairie, Cinderella,* and so on. Focus class discussion on how the characters in these and other books could be portrayed through the use of clothing and such items as hats, wigs, scarfs, shawls, costume jewelry, eyeglasses, umbrellas, and canes. Ask students to think about what items of clothing could be used to portray a geographical area, a historical period, a job or profession, or a "traditional" character such as a clown, witch, pirate, or princess.

## SELECTING CHARACTERS

If the project is to involve several classes or the whole school, there may be some additional considerations in selecting characters. Some classes may wish to represent a particular type of character according to a current or recent area of study. Some possibilities include biographical characters, characters from a particular historical period, characters from fairy tales or folklore, characters from poetry, or characters from many different books by one author. It's best to have students "sign up" for a character no later than one week before the date of the parade so that you can identify those who are having difficulty selecting a character and who may need advice.

## PLANNING COSTUMES

Once students have selected their characters, they will need to make lists of the items necessary to portray these characters. A sample list might be: "Cinderella—blackened dress, torn slippers, old shawl, scrub brush, pail." Students will need to decide which of the items on their lists they are likely to be able to borrow and which they will need to make. For those items that students construct themselves, try to have on hand such materials as brown paper bags, large and small cardboard boxes, old sheets, pillow cases, felt-tip markers, masking tape, etc. Students might also find ideas from books on simple costume making. The school librarian may be helpful in suggesting titles. Some possibilities are:

*Disguises You Can Make* by Eve Barwell
*Easy Costumes You Don't Have to Sew* by Goldie Taub Chernoff
*Costumes for Plays and Playing* by Gail E. Haley
*Easy-to-Make Costumes* by Frieda Gates
*Easy-to-Make Monster Masks and Disguises* by Frieda Gates

Encourage students to discuss their costume ideas and to help each other plan and prepare their own costumes.

To clearly indicate the identity of the characters and the books they came from, students might want to make character name tags or small signs to be worn during the parade. In addition, students might want to carry a copy of the chosen book. Another option is for students to prepare riddles about the chosen characters and to write the riddles on pieces of paper that are then pinned to the backs of their costumes. For example, a student dressed as Benjamin Franklin might wear the following note: "I helped write the Declaration of Independence. I was also an inventor. You can find my biography in the encyclopedia under F."

## PARADING THROUGH SCHOOL

The way you organize the parade will depend on the physical arrangement of the school, the number of classes and students involved, the ages of the students participating, and the preferences of those involved in the planning. In small schools, one class may be selected to lead the parade through the other classrooms, with each class joining the parade. If parents and others are assembled to watch, the parade would proceed to the assembly area where the program, announcements, or introductions would take place. In larger schools where there are several classes in each grade level, the parade could take place over a period of a few days or a week, with each grade parading on a different day.

## FOLLOWING UP

Books represented in the parade can be displayed in the classroom or library afterward, along with other books by the same authors or on related topics.

A story parade lends itself to follow-up discussions and writing assignments. You might ask students to describe their favorite costumes or to talk about how they would feel about really meeting some of the characters from the parade. Inspired by the parade, students might be interested in writing about the meetings of book characters—imagining, for instance, what Benjamin Franklin and Paul Bunyan might have to talk about, or how Tom Sawyer and Laura Ingalls Wilder would get along if they met.

*Marcia W. Purcifull, Brentwood School, Gainesville, Florida*

# ENACTING AND DIALOGUING

Students in an upper level elementary class have just finished a six-week unit on bridges, in which *Bridge to Terabithia* by Katherine Patterson was the literature selection.

Some examples of the Language Arts activities facilitated by the teacher were small groups that reread and reenacted a scene from their favorite part of the book and a whole class "hot seat" dialogue where various students took turns being the main character, "Jess." From the main character's point of view, the student had to answer questions from the audience regarding particular actions and decisions "Jess" made throughout the story, and the students also worked in pairs to rewrite and present a dialogue between two or more characters in the story.

For a final class presentation students had a choice of working individually, with a partner, or in a small group to present one of the above activities to the class. The teacher worked with the group to establish criteria for assessing performances. Items considered included volume, eye contact, clarity, fluency, accuracy of the presentation, etc.

As a reflection assignment, students wrote down why they picked their method of presentation and how they felt about their performance.

*Central California Council of Teachers of English Task Force, Oakland, CA*

# EXTENDING CHILDREN'S LITERATURE ACROSS THE CURRICULUM

## WHY

- To integrate classroom activities around literature
- To extend students' frame of reference from their closest immediate experiences and to move through concerns of the classroom, family, neighborhood, community, geographical area, and state to national and larger cultural issues and concerns

## HOW

The teacher uses a web framework (p. 80) to explore the many paths that children might take after studying one work of literature. As the children and teacher work together to make suggestions for the web, the teacher gets immediate feedback on children's reactions to the particular activities suggested.

The web is presented as a way of organizing children's experiences around Mercer Mayer's *What Do You Do with a Kangaroo?* The inner boxes list activities closest to the students' immediate experiences; the outer boxes involve more distant experiences.

*Robert C. Wortman, Tucson Unified School District, Arizona*

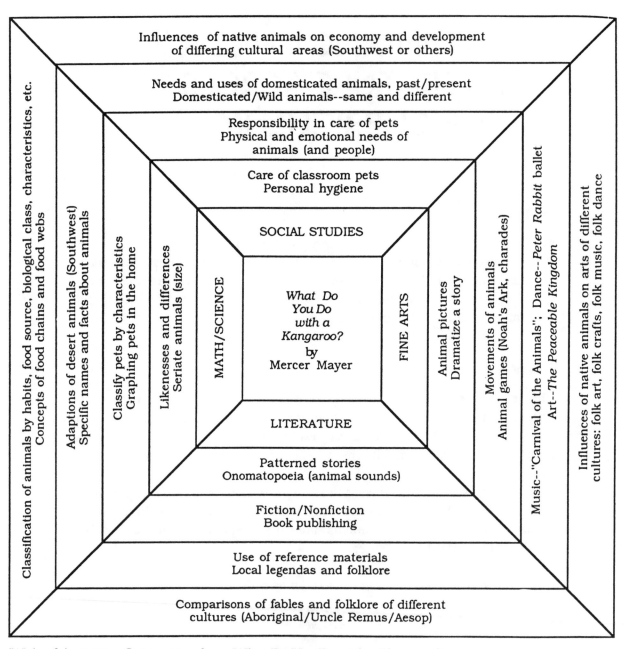

Web of Activities Originating from *What Do You Do with a Kangaroo?*

# LITERATURE RESPONSE SHEETS

Many times a well-written story will so involve children that they want to "respond" to the characters, scenes, or events. This means choosing their own forms of response. Some like talking, some prefer writing, others choose drawing, while still others enjoy singing or dancing.

In one part of the classroom, set up a Reading Response Corner. After students have read particular stories or books, they move to this corner to choose individual responses. One response they may choose is a printed "literature response sheet" that asks for art or a drawing to illustrate something from the book.

For example, on the handout sheet on page 82, the lens of the camera can be used to draw an event or a character. The transparent gift sack on page 83 gives space to draw a gift for one of the characters. Remind students they do not have to be artists to sketch people, places, or objects.

Response sheets to encourage a variety of drawings might include:

a medal (for a main character) to be decorated in an appropriate way
a crystal ball with space to draw a scene from one character's future
an empty picture frame or photo album to depict a memorable scene

Encourage students to share their drawings with each other. Also, be sure to provide blank sheets so students feel free to design their own response sheets.

*Arlene M. Pillar, Executive Enrichment System, New York, New York*

Directions: This camera gives you a close-up view of a happening or a character in the book you just read. Draw a picture of an event or character of your choice in the lens; then tell about your picture in your own words on the reverse side of this paper.

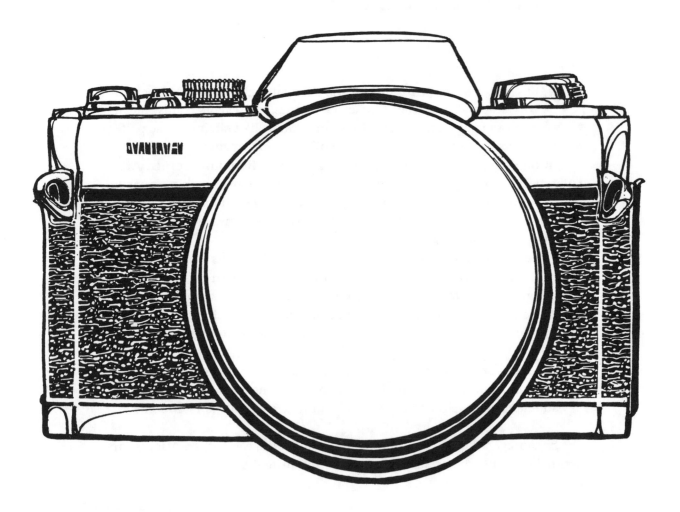

Your name_____
Date_____
Book title_____
Author_____

Directions: This transparent gift sack holds a special gift for one of the characters in the book you just read. Pick a character and decide what gift you'd like to give that character. Then draw the item inside the sack. On the reverse side of this paper, tell the name of the character who will receive the gift and explain why you chose this gift.

Your name_____

Date_____

Book title_____

Author_____

# GAMES BASED ON CHILDREN'S LITERATURE

## WHY

- To encourage students to use predicting strategies
- To broaden students' vocabulary
- To expand students' knowledge of sentence structure
- To emphasize literature in the reading program

## HOW

### Game Board

Invite students to select a favorite book or story. Make a game board out of poster board, mat board, oaktag, or cardboard, and design a pattern of spaces for playing pieces to occupy. The book or story might determine the shape of the spaces, such as foot shapes for a game based on Tomie de Paola's *Now One Foot, Now the Other.* For the spaces, include three alternating colors that will be color-coded to the activities that accompany the game. Not all spaces need to be color-coded—some can be "free" spaces where no activity occurs. Spaces can be colored, painted, or made from colored paper pasted to the board. Be sure to consider storage, cost, durability, and attractiveness when choosing materials for your games.

### Cloze Cards

These cards encourage students to predict language. Choose one of the colors used on the game board, and cut the cloze cards in any uniform size and shape. These cards will become one of the decks for playing the game. Select a sentence or short passage from the book. Print or type the selection on a card, omitting one key word and leaving a blank space in its place. Make all the blanks the same length so that readers will use meaning as their strategy in determining the missing word rather than counting letters. Two sample cloze sentences are shown below.

> "Now, tell me the story about how you _____ me to walk,"
>    Bobby said.
> Bobby was named after his best _____, his grandfather, Bob.

Make several more cloze cards than the number of spaces your game board has in that color. During the game, players landing on a space of that color will draw a cloze card, read the card aloud, and fill in the blank with the word from the book or a word that makes just as much sense. The other players decide if substitutions are acceptable, meaningful language. The player will advance a predetermined number of spaces if the other players agree on the appropriateness of the response.

### Meaning Cards

Prepare a second deck of cards, selecting another color on the game board. Cut the cards in any desirable size or shape. Again, select phrases or sentences from the text of the book or story. Print or type each selection from the book onto a card, underlining one word or phrase significant to the meaning of the story. Sentences from two sample meaning cards are shown below.

> Sometimes the <u>tower</u> would be almost finished.

> And they would <u>carefully</u> put the elephant block on the very top.

Players landing on a space of that color will draw a meaning card from this color deck, read the card aloud, and explain what the underlined word means in relation to the rest of the text. Responses must meet with the satisfaction of the players.

### Language Strips

Cut strips of paper to match the remaining color on the game board. Select sentences or paragraphs from the book and print or type one selection on each strip. Cut each sentence or paragraph strip into two, three, four, or five segments, depending on its length and on the sophistication of the children (longer segments for younger children), and clip the segments together. When students land on a space of this color, their task is to reconstruct a meaningful text to the satisfaction of all the players. For example, a student would need to rearrange the following segments:

> the fireworks.
> And when it got
> dark, they watched

into this sentence:

And when it got dark, they watched the fireworks.

### General Procedure

To regulate movement in the game, use a game spinner or die from another game, or make a game die from a sponge cube. Decide on the maximum number of players for the game and provide as many different playing pieces to move around the game board, using buttons, corks, small toy cars, or other toy pieces. Taking turns, players move their playing pieces around the board according to the spinner or die and then must answer a question from the deck of cards that matches the space their playing piece is occupying. The winner is the player who completes the game-board circuit first or who answers the most questions correctly.

Write an instruction sheet or card that can be read and understood clearly by students. Make this and all game pieces more permanent by laminating them or covering them with clear adhesive-backed paper.

## WHAT ELSE

Invite children to construct games for their own class as well as for younger children.

*Wendy C. Kasten, University of South Florida at Sarasota*

# PLANNING YOUR OWN YOUNG AUTHORS' CONFERENCE

## PURPOSE

- To talk to a published author
- To gain confidence in one's own writing
- To enjoy reading and writing

## MATERIALS

- Paper, pencils, posterboard, colored markers
- Copies of the guest author's book(s), two portable tables, folding chairs
- Microphone (optional)

An encounter with a published author can make the experience of reading and writing more meaningful for your students. With the general guidelines below, and a little volunteer help, you can treat the students in your school to their own "Young Authors' Conference" and help them to take their own reading and writing more seriously.

## FINDING AN AUTHOR

First find a willing children's author living within a reasonable distance of your community. Librarians and booksellers can help you to decide upon and contact potential guest authors; often they can be reached by addressing a letter in care of their publisher. The best-known authors require higher fees and may need to be booked a year in advance, but new writers are often eager to talk with students about their work and may agree to come for the cost of travel expenses and the opportunity to sell a few books. Once you have found a willing author, select a mutually convenient date and start to plan. A few weeks before the conference date, remember to send your guest author a copy of the conference day's schedule and the name of the teacher or parent volunteer who will be emceeing the event(s).

## FUNDING

Estimate the total cost of your conference. Include:

- Fees for your guest author (honorarium, travel, accommodations, meals)
- Materials for workshops (paper, pencils, books, optional refreshments)
- Printing costs (if you plan to print a program, posters, or collections of writings by students who attend)
- Expenditures for phone calls and mailings (including reminder notices to parents)

If school funds are available, great! If not, there are alternatives. For example, your local parent-teacher organization may be willing to contribute, and your local library or library association might be interested in "joint sponsorship" of the guest author. You can also request donations from community organizations, local businesses, or the community newspaper. Be sure to give your sponsors credit wherever possible—on programs, posters, advertisements, etc.

## ORDERING BOOKS

Select popular, affordable titles by the guest author and estimate how many books you can sell. Order books directly from the children's book division of the publisher, or enlist the help of your local bookstore for this purpose. You may be able to obtain a discount from the publisher for a quantity purchase.

## PLANNING THE DAY

Your Young Authors' Conference can be simple—or not so simple. You and fellow teachers will need to decide what your resources—time, money, space, and parent helpers—will allow.

Include a general assembly during which the guest author talks, answers questions, and interacts with students. You might want to follow the assembly with book-sharing sessions in which students read their own writings to an audience of their peers. Or you may even want to offer workshops conducted by teachers and librarians on topics such as poetry, personal narrative, journalism, bookbinding, anything that seems appropriate.

Someone, a teacher or a parent, will need to emcee the day's activities, even if this only involves introducing the guest author at the assembly. And you'll need to arrange for a teacher or willing parent to sell the author's books at a book table by the door on the day of the conference.

You will also need to set aside a time and a place for book signing. Seek the advice of your prospective guest, since some authors have a preference as to how book signing is conducted.

Make sure you enlist volunteers to mix the punch or set out crackers and cheese if you decide to serve refreshments.

## PUBLICITY

Don't forget to publicize your conference. Advise your local newspaper and radio and television stations that an important event will take place in your school, and invite them to attend. Good publicity benefits your school as well as the guest author.

## PREPARING STUDENTS

To gain the most from the guest author's visit, students should read and discuss as much of the author's work as possible beforehand. A month or two before the conference, obtain several copies of each of the author's books. Prepare sign-up sheets for each title. As students check off their names, they look to see who else has finished the same book. These students then get together to share reactions to characters, settings, and plots. Tell students that once they have a feeling for the author's style, they should make notes on questions they want to ask the author.

Students may also want to prepare something to share with the author in response to his or her work. This could be anything from a description of the student's reaction to a character to a story or drawing inspired by one of the author's books.

Set aside several additional class periods for students to:

- Make Young Authors' Conference posters to be displayed in the classroom and around the school
- Polish their writings in preparation for a group read-aloud session

About a month before the conference date mimeograph an invitation to be mailed to parents and students.

## PREPARATION ON THE DAY

You and your "aides" for the day, other teachers and parent volunteers, should arrive several hours before the assembly to make sure that chairs are in place and to set up two tables (one for selling books and one for signing them). The guest author will want to arrive early too, if he or she has any display materials to arrange. Place a jar of pens on the book-signing table, set up the microphone if you are providing one, and then sit back and wait for the participants.

Lastly, enjoy your conference. And rest assured that your young authors will remember this day for a long time to come!

*Wendy C. Kasten, Sarasota, Florida*

# | PIONEER PROJECT

## PURPOSE

- To practice reading
- To choose main events from reading
- To write chapter summaries
- To learn about the lives of early pioneers
- To write descriptively

## MATERIALS

- Copies of *Little House on the Prairie* by Laura Ingalls Wilder
- Study prints and maps showing the routes traveled by the pioneers
- A copy of *Children of the Wild West* by Russell Freedman
- Large sheets of brown paper for murals
- Pencils, colored markers, crayons, scissors, and glue

When a book captures the interest of students who don't normally like to read, it seems like a good idea to capitalize on that interest. It was with that purpose in mind that I sought out additional resources and related activities to expand our class reading of Laura Ingalls Wilder's *Little House on the Prairie.* Through this informally structured project, my remedial fourth graders, most of them reading on a second-grade level, read and enjoyed the entire book in a period of several months. In the meantime, they learned both about the author's life as a pioneer child in Missouri and about pioneer life in general. Students' enthusiasm for *Little House on the Prairie* was such that we decided to take a few extra weeks and learn to write "like Laura Ingalls Wilder."

As we read and discussed the first chapters of the book, we took time out every few days to look through study prints depicting pioneer life. (The set we used was "Pioneer Days," distributed by Fideler Visual Teaching.) Our fourth-grade social studies curriculum focuses on local history, so when students began reading *Little House on the Prairie,* they had already begun to learn about the pioneer families who first settled our own county. In our discussions about the reading, I encouraged students to draw parallels between the experiences of those early settlers and the experiences of the Ingalls.

Maps were a useful supplement to reading. Using a map of the United States in an atlas, I helped students locate our own state, county, and city. Then we traced the probable route taken by the Ingalls as they traveled from the big woods of Wisconsin, across the Mississippi River, and down south to Missouri, where they settled about forty miles from Independence. We also looked at a map, included with the study prints, that showed all of the major routes followed by pioneers traveling west. Class discussion that day touched on how the Ingalls travel in *Little House on the Prairie.* In one chapter, the author describes how the family rides across a solidly frozen river on the ice. The next night they hear sounds like the report of a rifle, indicating that the ice is cracking. Students excitedly made the inference Wilder intended the family had gotten across the river just in time and might have drowned if they had tried to cross any later. This led to a discussion of how the author, by skillfully providing clues, made the telling of the incident particularly exciting.

Another valuable resource was a book of antique photographs titled *Children of the Wild West* by Russell Freedman, which depicted actual pioneer life. As we read and discussed the book, we realized that pioneers were not necessarily as lighthearted or as attractive as they are presented to be on television. Photographs of the pioneer men, women, and children and of the Native American families they displaced reveal careworn faces, patched and worn clothing, and gnarled hands, and suggest that they endured a lot of hard work. Also shown are "stick and daub" chimneys, daguerreotypes of wagon boxes slung with all manner of household utensils, and other features of pioneer life. Students carefully examined the photographs and pointed out things they recognized from Wilder's descriptions.

On another day, I asked students to brainstorm ways in which the lives of the pioneer children were different from their own lives in the present. Students mentioned danger, lack of doctors and medicine, being less protected from the weather, having fewer games and sports to play and more work to do, and, conversely, excitement, challenges, being treated more like an adult, being outdoors more, and being able to grow or hunt your own food and make your own clothes and shelter. The long list of differences I copied onto the chalkboard sparked a heated discussion among my students as to whether they would rather live in the present time or when the pioneers lived. Although the conflict was never resolved, the discussion helped students develop a more realistic picture of what was involved in pioneer life.

The final chapters of *Little House on the Prairie* describe relations among the white settlers and the various Native American tribes that were displaced by the westward movement. Several scenes show the angry and frustrated behavior of certain tribespeople and the fearful, prejudiced reactions of some of the settlers. When students had reached this point in their reading, I introduced a historical account of the period from the book *Children of the Wild West.* Photographs and captions show how some Native Americans were encouraged to give up their dress, language, and customs in order to live among the whites. My students were able to empathize with the problems faced by the Native Americans due in part to the sensitive way these issues were handled by Wilder in her book.

About three quarters of the way through our reading of the book, we began working on murals depicting important events in the story. We planned our scenes on the chalkboard before sketching anything on butcher paper. Some students worked on the background setting, drawing grass, covered wagons, a stream, and trees. These were then colored with markers and crayons. Other students sketched the figures of the people, horses, and the dog on white drawing paper. These were colored, cut out, and glued onto the mural to give a little more depth to the scene. Captions and titles were lettered on the mural where necessary.

When the murals were completed and students were almost finished with their reading, I asked students to write short summaries of the chapters, including the events pictured in our murals. We worked on the summary for the first chapter as a group, referring to the book to select important events. The process of summarizing included lively discussions on whether certain aspects of the scene were main events or only details.

By the time the school year neared an end, we had completed five large murals and hung them in the corridor of the school. Students were proud of having completed the book and were busy revising and proofreading their chapter summaries. But when these summaries were completed, students still weren't ready to stop talking about Laura Ingalls Wilder. So, with three weeks left in the school year, we began discussing Laura Ingalls Wilder's writing style. We talked about the details that she used in her writing and her skill in creating suspense with words. Wilder's biography in the basal reader stated that she wrote about what she really knew and that this partly explained the appeal of her books. My students agreed that they would like to try to write like Laura Ingalls Wilder.

Students chose to write about incidents from their own lives, as Wilder did. To help students include interesting details, I asked them to prepare "idea sheets." They divided sheets of paper into six columns and labeled these columns *see, hear, smell, taste, touch,* and *feelings.* Then they listed appropriate details in each column and used these details to begin their first drafts.

Many students began with a paragraph emphasizing sensory details and followed it with a paragraph that concentrated on the sequence of events and what happened. They had discovered this pattern repeatedly in *Little House on the Prairie.* Many students also attempted to keep their readers in suspense the way Wilder did. When students had revised and proofread their drafts, they illustrated their descriptions and mounted them on colored paper. I displayed the stories near the murals, accompanied by a sign that said, "These students have learned to write like Laura Ingalls Wilder."

*Edythe R. Shapiro, Mechanicstown School, Middletown, New York*